企業と社会フォーラム学会誌　第 10 号

JN013989

編集：企業と社会フォーラム　　　発行：千倉書房

目　次

は じ め に

　学会「企業と社会フォーラム」（JFBS）は，2011 年に発足し今年 10 周年を迎えた。それを記念して本誌では巻頭に Joachim Schwalbach フンボルト大学教授と Timothy M. Devinney マンチェスター大学教授による招待論文 "Corporate Purpose: Fact or Fiction?　Myth or Reality? The Honourable Merchant as the Historic Basis of Corporate Purpose" を掲載している。JFBS は，Schwalbach 教授がリードしてきた International Conference on Sustainability and Responsibility と連携してきた。Devinney 教授は同大会 Committee メンバーとして支えてこられ，Academy of Management Perspectives の Co-Editor も勤められた。論文は，混迷する時代において改めて企業のパーパスを問い直し，企業（家）とは何かを考え直す契機を与えてくれる。

　本号では，さらに本年 3 月に行われた企画シンポジウム「日本におけるポストコロナと持続可能な『企業と社会』」の抄録，事例紹介・解説，学界展望から構成されている。当初第 10 号は，昨年9 月に開催予定であった第 10 回年次大会での議論およびその後の研究成果をもとにした論文を所収する予定であった。しかし，新型コロナウイルス感染症の影響により大会の開催が中止，延期となったため，それらは次号に持ち越しとなった。

　ところで，JFBS は 2020-2021 年，コロナ禍によって対面での大会，研究会ができなくなったことに対応し，オンラインでの研究会およびシンポジウムを積極的に開催してきた。これまでは東京に来ることが難しかったスピーカーや参加者がオンライン参加することができ，多様な議論を展開することができた。とくにコロナ禍における企業と社会にかかわる問題について，2 つのシンポジウムを企画し，国際的にあるいはセクター横断的に考え議論してきた。

　国際シンポジウム "Sustainability Management in Post Corona Era"（1 月 23 日）においては，ロシア，韓国，タイ，インドネシア，台湾からスピーカーを迎え，コロナ禍は企業活動にどのような影響を及ぼしたのか，各国において企業はステイクホルダーと今後どのような関係を構築していけばよいのか，議論を行った。もう一つ，シンポジウム「日本におけるポストコロナと持続可能な『企業と社会』」（3 月 6 日）においては，日本ではポストコロナにおいて何が問い直され，何がこれまでと変わらないのか，企業セクター，NGO セクターの実務家と研究者が多様な視点から議論を行った（本誌抄録参照）。

　投稿論文に関しては，JFBS 編集委員会による審査が行われた。今回国内外から投稿された学術論文 3 本については，残念ながら最終的に掲載に至らなかった。事例紹介・解説については投稿された 4 本のうち 3 本が掲載されることとなった。今後とも学術論文の積極的な投稿を期待している。

　学界展望は，JFBS が設立 10 周年を迎えたことを記念して，この 10 年間の活動を総括し，次の10 年に向けた課題を示している。

　さて，本年 9 月に開催される第 10 回年次大会では「サーキュラーエコノミーを目指して」

（Circular Economy Transition: Exploring the Institutional, Organizational & Behavioral Dimensions）を
テーマとし，持続可能な経済社会の実現に向けた理論構築，政府の政策や企業の経営戦略の策定，
セクターを超えたコラボレーションなど，広く議論を行う予定である。具体的には，プラスチック
問題，食品ロス，サステナブルファッション，再生可能エネルギー，持続可能な農業，シェアリン
グなど多くの課題が問われることになる。

　コロナ禍の中，今後の動向が読めないため，第10回大会は全面オンラインで開催することと
なった。10回記念大会のキーノートスピーカーの一人として，ステイクホルダー理論で有名な
ヴァージニア大学のEdward Freeman教授をお呼びしている。大会の内容や申し込みについて
は，JFBSのウエブサイトを参照いただきたい（https://j-fbs.jp）。

　最後に，コロナ感染の一日も早い収束を願うとともに，多くの研究者，実務家が安心して集ま
り，再び活発な議論ができるようになることを願っている。
　今号も発行に当たっては千倉書房に大変お世話になった。記して感謝の意を表したい。

2021年6月

企業と社会フォーラム会長
早稲田大学商学学術院商学部教授
谷本　寛治

Japan Forum of Business and Society Annals, No.10, pp. 1-13, 2021   1

Corporate Purpose: Fact or Fiction? Myth or Reality?

——The Honourable Merchant as the Historic Basis of Corporate Purpose

Timothy M. Devinney

Chair and Professor of International Business

Alliance Manchester Business School

University of Manchester

Joachim Schwalbach

Professor emeritus of International Management

School of Business and Economics

Humboldt-Universität zu Berlin

Key words : Core Function of the Corporation, Corporate Purpose, Strategy and Governance, Principles of Honourable Merchant, Responsible Leadership, Self-Responsibility, Corporate Responsibility, Sustainable Business, Relationship between Business and Society

【Abstract】

Since the financial market crisis of 2008, the call for responsible corporate management has become both louder and broader. The politicians, activists and ordinary citizens in many countries fear that existing corporate control mechanisms might not be enough to put a stop to financial gamblers in what they perceive as a societal ethics-void. To this extent, the financial crisis revealed both societal and corporate deficiencies in the basic understanding of responsible, sustainable, honourable and thus successful, corporate leadership.

The paper shows that Corporate Purpose and the principles of Honourable Merchants coincide and come into play. The guiding principles assume that responsible behaviour enacted by those in leadership position is the basis for sustainable economic success and social peace in society. While much of this had been lost as social responsibility became more codified in law rather than driven by practice and collective value, today we may be seeing a move back from legal doctrine to moral suasion and collective value based action.

Although the corporation as a form dates from the 17th Century, what we would call the "modern corporation" originated with the development of formal corporate law, and the establishment of limited liability, in the middle of the 19th Century. However, up until the early 20th century there was little discussion as to whom a corporation was ultimately responsible. While historically corporations would be chartered by the state (or the ruler) and hence their "license to operate" (LTO) would be subject to the rights of the state (or the whims of the ruler), this regulatory oversight has devolved to a wide variety of jurisdictions over time.

In *The Theory of Moral Sentiments*, Adam Smith laid out a socio political philosophy as to the nature of people's personal, political and economic interactions. In something a counter balance to *The Wealth of Nations*, Smith argues that there is more to personal and commercial interaction than just self-interest: "*How selfish soever man may be supposed, there are evidently some principles in his nature, which interest him in the fortune of others, and render their happiness necessary to him, though he derives nothing from it, except the pleasure of seeing it*" (The Theory of Moral Sentiments, I, §I, Ch. I, p. 9). Smith talks about two guides to decision making, rules and virtues. Rules serve as the core of regulation of actions and articulate what is and is not permitted in a society. Virtue, however, goes beyond simply following the rules and reflects not just 'intentions' but the 'consequences' of decisions and actions on others. From a corporate perspective, what mostly mattered to the operation of the corporation were "rules" as opposed to "virtues".

It was really not until the famous Berle-Dodd debates of the 1930s (see, e.g., A. Sommer, Jr. [1991], Whom Should the Corporation Serve – The Berle-Dodd Debate Revisited Sixty Years Later, *Delaware Corp Law Journal*) that the idea that someone other than the owners of the firm (i.e., the shareholders or private owners) had legal and regulatory rights moved into mainstream policy and legal discussions. If we fast forward this debate into the latter part of the 20th Century, Freeman (*Strategic Management: A Stakeholder Approach*) argued that there are more claimants on corporate rights and that the best corporations are those that recognize and manage the complexities of those diverse and competing claimants, whom he call "stakeholders". Today, the debate has progressed further, where regulators, investors, stakeholders and managers all recognize there is an implicit (and sometimes increasingly explicit) "Social License to Operate" (SLTO) that goes far beyond the traditional and narrowly legal LTO that has been the commercial norm. In Smith's parlance, we have moved from an era where "rules" alone mattered to one in which corporations are now required to live by the rules and to act virtuously.

This leads us to the rather recent notion of **corporate purpose**. The key to corporate purpose is to recognize that the core function of the corporation is not to make money, nor is that the ultimate goal. The making of money is the result of a whole series of technologies, processes, decisions, and so on that lead to the most appropriate and desirable outcome to a collective of stakeholders who both co-create value and willingly share the value created in what is recognized as a fair distribution.

The logic of corporate purpose is sometimes difficult to see with respect to large public corporations who ultimately get captured by standardize internal processes, investor benchmarks and an increasing distance from their point of founding. However, the idea of purpose is more visible with smaller enterprises or firms where a family or single individual is the driving force. When questioned these individuals rarely say they went into business to make money. Invariably, there was another passion that drove them to do what they did. Sometimes the initial purpose was an expediency. As Steve Jobs noted about the beginnings of Apple: *"Basically Steve Wozniak and I invented the Apple because we wanted a personal computer. Not only couldn't we afford the computers that were on the market, those computers were impractical for us to use."* Similarly, Ben & Jerry's founded an ice cream company because making bagels was too expensive and Ben (Cohen) had a condition that made it hard for him to smell (hence their trademark 'chunks' in the ice cream). For these organizations, the purpose is their raison d'être. It becomes internalized in terms of processes and goals and, if successful, is the motivator for employees down the line. As we will note shortly, purpose can also reflect an internalization of a potential public good in a more generalized sense, should all organizations choose to align with a "code of conduct" that embodies shared values.

1. | Corporate Purpose as Strategy & Governance in the Modern Corporation

But how does the notion of corporate purpose apply to the large public corporation. In this instance, we can look at two aspects – strategy and governance.

Richard Rumelt distinguishes between "bad strategy" – a strategy that "accommodate[s] a multitude of conflicting demands and inter-

ests" – and "good strategy" that focuses "energy and resources on one, or a very few, pivotal objectives whose accomplishment will lead to a cascade of favorable outcomes". Having a clear and distinctive purpose, as opposed to a plethora of goals and key performance indicators (KPIs) unique to divisions and subsidiaries, can be the essence of a good strategy. It makes clear the line of sight between the purpose and actions/decisions as the key question is simply "how does this action/decision enable us to fulfill our purpose?" It also aligns any subsidiary KPIs to a singular point of reference. For employees it means that the do not need to be driven by rules but by virtue. As Herb Kelleher, the late CEO of Southwest Airlines put it, *"If you create an environment where the people truly participate, you don't need control. They know what needs to be done and they do it."* The key, of course, is to have a meaningful and actionable purpose that resonates distinctly and operationally with the key stakeholders.

The key to successful governance is also driven by purpose. The legal requirements of board members fall clearly into the category of rules. Some boards work well, and others do not. But whether they work well or not has almost nothing to do with whether or not they know the rules and choose to follow them or not. We are all schooled in the rules that define "hard governance". What matters is "soft governance" – the unwritten rules, routines and interactions that embody the underlying culture of the organization. It is what people do about the rules and what they do when there are no rules, or the rules are unclear or provide no guidance. In other words, it is the virtues aspect of governance. The key to governance is the fact that virtues flow downward – the board and top management team embody them and their choices and decisions and modes of speaking, interacting and managing signal what is virtuous and purposeful. If they do not live the purpose of the organization, purpose becomes shallow and meaningless.

So why is purpose important? Today organizations are facing three existential threats. The first is related to climate and it impact on businesses and societies. The second is public health, most noticeably seen in the case of Covid-19 but seen in other major outbreaks and systemic health issues related to lifestyle and longevity. The third is the failure of political governance and the rise of populist leaders in both democratic and autocratic political systems. Together they force companies into decision making modes for which clear options are not there. If you are HSBC, how do you deal with the Hong Kong Security Law? If you are Google or Facebook, how do you deal with calls for data protection, transparency and hate speech? Or demands for back door access by security agencies? If you are any multinational enterprise how do you address demands for local taxation or the outsourcing of operations? If you are a pharmaceutical company working on a Covid-19 vaccine, how do you address issues of access, pricing and efficacy of the treatment? For any company, what is your commitment to climate action over and above aspects that might be considered "greenwash"?

The list of questions for which the answers are not clear is nearly endless. But what is clear is that there are no simple business model answers to them. It is also clear that the answers to questions like these are not only strategic but critical to the head-to-toe aspects of any business. So you have a series of questions for which there is no guidance and as a board or senior executive you have to signal to the rest of your organization that the decisions you are making are more than just compromises that satisfy no one and reflect nothing truly. It is here where purpose matters. If there is a clear purpose to the organization, reflected in the virtues that underly all that motivates the individuals in that organization, the answers become clearer. They may no be crystal clear, but purpose helps highlight what actions can be ruled out. Google reflected this when it chose not to compromise with the Chinese governments demands for censorship and handed over that market to competitors.

But it is important to recognize that purpose may be reflected in values but that it is more. Companies compromise on supposed values all the time and most companies list of values amount to little more than generic motherhood statements. They make commitments to employees but engage in outsourcing and retrenchment. They make commitments to customers but raise prices when it is convenient. They make commitments to suppliers but change them all the time. They make commitments to the environment or social causes but rarely beyond a limited impact on their business model.

Hence, purpose matters when it is simple. Purpose matters when it is embodied by the board and top management team. Purpose matters when it directs operational and financial KPIs. Purpose matters when every decision can be justified as an alignment to the purpose. Purpose matters when it is lived by each and every employee and understood and respected by all the organization's stakeholders.

2. | Honourable Merchants: Corporate Purpose in Germany's Midsize Hidden Champions

Germany's small and mid-size companies, known as the Mittelstand, have been recognized as particularly unique champions of global competition. Yet, despite their success they have remained mainly hidden in their market niches. Hermann Simon has studied these hidden champions extensively and characterized them as embracing five common practices (Simon, 1992):

(1) Combine strategic focus with geographic diversity.

(2) Emphasize factors like customer value.

(3) Blend technology and closeness to customers.

(4) Rely on their own technical competence.

(5) Create mutual interdependence between the company and its employees.

If you delve into the history of the corporate purpose of these hidden champions you come across the Principles of Honourable Merchants (PHM), which is embedded in the German economic system known as the "Soziale Marktwirtschaft". As we, will discuss here, this structure reflects more than corporate purpose alone but reflects an industrial internalization of common purpose that self regulates via historic precedent.

The PHM have, as will be shown, a thousand-year tradition that has reflected a remarkable resiliency. A variety of economic crises – such as the bursting of the dotcom bubble 2000/01, the financial market crisis in 2007/8 and numerous subsequent business scandals (for instance: Enron 2001 in the U.S. and most recently Wirecard in Germany) – have reinforced and revitalized the PHM. The 'Assembly of an Honourable Merchant to Hamburg' celebrated in 2017 its 500th anniversary as the largest and oldest association of ethical businessmen in Germany.

In fact, as late as 2017, the PHM incorporated into the German Corporate Governance Code (DCGK) which "highlights the obligation of Management and Supervisory Boards to ensure the continued existence of the company and its sustainable value creation in line with the principles of the social market economy.... These principles not only require compliance with law, but also ethically sound and responsible behaviour" (DCGK, 2017).

In economics, the PHM are embedded in the wider research area of Corporate Social Responsibility (CSR) (Devinney et al. 2013) which focuses on the relationship between current economic and social policy as well as business and it promotes measures to oblige companies to develop their own responses towards such policy as well as to regularly communicate (positive as well as negative) impacts of their business activity on the economy, the environment and society.

Members of the Mittelstand explicitly refer their corporate purpose to the PHM. For instance, the German family company Trumpf GmbH + Co. KG, largest producer of Machine Tools and global leader for Laser Technology, explicitly follow the PHM, by stating:

> *I am convinced that the question of the future of the honourable merchant is decided by his personal actions. Through his actions, he must demonstrate the maxims according to which he leads his life. His example is decisive. Reliability is decisive. ...Credibility is the highest asset to be acquired. .... We need ... the honourable businessman because human coexistence, if it is to function, is based on mutual trust, even across national and cultural borders* (Berthold Leibinger, 2006).

3. The History of Honourable Merchants

For the understanding of the principles of Honourable Merchants and for the assessment of the transferability to modern entrepreneurship, the historical genesis and evolution of the *Principles* are of central importance. The following section explores the millennium of the *Principles of Honourable Merchants* and transforms these into a contemporary model of corporate responsibility towards society.

The concept of honour is the focus of the leitmotif *Honourable Merchant*. The term "Merchant" is used as a substitute for the individu-

als that self-employed, entrepreneur, and/or manager.

The concept of honour is not an absolute concept. It is strongly subject to historical change. Honour is often defined in two dimensions: **external honour** – as the evaluation of the individual shaped by the environment and social context – and the **inner honour** – as the sense of honour perceived by the individual himself. The duality of the term is part of the stability of the concept. In fact, this concept can be traced back usefully to ancient times with Aristotle suggesting in *Nicomachean Ethics*: "Honour is the triumph of virtue and is given only to the good" (Aristotle 2005: 85). Considering honour as a reward of virtue, proposes external honour to be dependent on the inner. Virtue is understood by Aristotle as a behaviour "between two wickedness; excess and deficiency" (ibid.: 42). Honour is not a single virtue of many; it is the result of the applied virtues of the individual and it becomes an expression of its value, which in turn resonates with the values of the epoch. Hence an honourable person is tied to virtues: If the practiced values of the individual are recognised externally by the community, it can be said to represent external honour. If an individual recognises and enacts his or her own values from inside, the person has an inner sense of self-worth, which is described as inner honour. This understanding of honour is the most useful as a basis for the consideration of the Honourable Merchants, as merchants always directly relate to the community whose members measure them in their conduct. Honour changes and represents itself in a dialectic process between the individual and the community.

4. | The Honourable Merchant in Antiquity

"Whoever is fair and true in the market, Zeus will give him wealth," says Hesiod of Askra in the Greek Boeotia around 700 BC. (Baloglou and Peukert 1996: 23). This is one of the oldest testimonies for Honourable Merchants in European history and illustrates that the behaviour of economic actors in markets has always been the subject of normative expressions. Particularly noteworthy is the combination of the desirable behavioural standard (fair, true) with the success (wealth).

Comparable statements exist throughout European history and are an expression of a deep-rooted culture of entitlement to entrepreneurial decency, which does not mean that European merchants have always lived up to this claim. Many negative examples speak a different language to this day, and doubts about reaching this ideal have also existed since ancient times.

Demosthenes, a Greek speaker and son of a manufacturer (Fellmeth 2008: 43), who, in 384–322 BC, found it difficult to find a man who did business and, at the same time, was industrious and Honourable (cf. Baloglou and Constantinides 1993: 61). He also observed that "in the business world and on the money market, it is admirable when the same man proves to be honest and diligent at the same time" (according to Fellmeth 2008: 42). Of course, this also means that there were always merchants who aspired to the ideal of honest merchants.

One of the first to make a name for himself in this context was the banker Pasion (from 400–370 BC) from Athens, who was "apparently very efficient and honest" (ibid.: 40) and was highly regarded in Athens. Economising with the goal of winning, as is typical for merchants, had already become sociable at Hesiod's time. But, as Demokrit (Greek philosopher, 460–370 BC) makes clear, "the acquisition of money is not useless, but unjustly it is worse than anything" (according to Baloglou and Constantinides 1993: 26).

It was well known to the Greeks that Honourable Merchants unite economy and ethics. A statement from the work "Oikonomíka", presumed to be written by a disciple of Aristotle in the 3rd century BC, confirms, however, the systematic linking of business skills and virtue, which is the basis of the success:

> *Those who want to do business in a dignified manner (oikonomein) must be aware of the places where they operate, and must be naturally endowed, as well as to spare no effort and justice on their own initiative. If something is missing from these qualities, he will make many mistakes in the projects he takes* (according to Fellmeth 2008: 8).

In fact, the concepts of Honourable Merchants were characterised by very early on by the acceptance of profit-making and economic performance criteria, but these had to be in harmony with its societal context of virtuous behaviour, so that the merchants could call themselves Honourable. Rome's decline and the time of the migration of the peoples led to a long period of European reorganisation and transition across very different societies, national and productive strictures where the principles of Honourable Merchants survived with few changes although Hesiod's godfather Zeus was replaced by the Christian faith in the European Middle Ages.

5. | The Honourable Merchant in the Middle Ages

The earliest source of Honourable Merchants in the Middle Ages can be traced back to the famous Italian handbook *Pratica della Mercatura*, published around 1340. There, Francesco Balducci Pegolotti reproduces in his introduction the verses of Dino Compagni (see Le Goff 1993: 85):

> *The merchant, who wants to enjoy respect, must always to act fairly, have great farsightedness and always keep his promises. If possible, he should look amiable, as the Honourable profession which he has chosen corresponds sincerely to the sale, be attentive to the purchase, he should thank him and keep distance from complaints. His prestige will be even greater when he visits the Church, for love of God, without haggling;*

Luca Pacioli (1445-1517), who is the inventor of double bookkeeping, writes in 1494, in the first chapter of his book *Summa De Arithmetica, Geometrica, Proportioni Et Proportionità*, that the three conditions of true merchants are: (1) the money, (2) a good calculator, and, (3) a proper accounting of the debt and the receivables (see Pacioli 1494). The merchants' manuals and Pacioli itself can be seen today as a precursor of management science and management textbooks. For example, double-entry bookkeeping still belongs to the basic knowledge of every student of economics, management and accounting, yet it is a system of calculation and record-keeping designed by merchants for their own control and for the assurance of the honest merchant's practice.

The virtuous behaviour complements the professional abilities of the merchants. The clerks of the merchant manuals were aware that ethical behavior and the good name of merchants were assets that had to be protected as well (Pacioli 1494: 84). The first truly detailed handbook is the *Zibaldone da Canal*, of Venetian origin, dated around 1320 (ibid.: 77). The *Zibaldone* expresses the consequences of smuggling as follows: "... you lose faith and honour by it, so that they will never trust you as before your crime was found out" (Zibaldone da Canal ca. 1320, after Dotson 2002: 84). By criminal machinations, merchants lost the trust and honour they placed in them and the long-term loss of reputation was a loss of such severity that criminal machinations were, literally, not worth it.

The Middle Ages already recognised the economic significance of the activity of the merchants. In fact, they had a great influence on the development of cities. Benedetto of Ragusa wrote in his handbook *Trade and the Ideal Merchant* in the 15th century: "The progress, the common good, and the prosperity of the States depend to a large extent on the merchants; [...]. The work of the merchants is arranged for the benefit of humanity" (see Benedetto, 15th century, according to Le Goff 1993: 80–81). In turn, merchants knew it was in their interest when they maintained social peace through charity (Le Goff 1993: 106). The city was the basis of its success, its business and its power and took the highest place in their reflections and considerations (cf. ibid.: 120). The merchants, as patrons, supported the literature and art within their city and regarded culture as indication of the city's success and their sponsorship as indication of their status in the success of the city.

While the surviving literature mainly refers to Italian merchants, there is a generalizability as to the bundle of virtues and good behaviours of merchants within the Christian community.

6. | The Honourable Merchant in the Early Modern Period

In the early modern period, religion largely disappeared as a source of understanding, interpretation and of guidance for individuals within communities (Le Goff 1993: 96). Throughout the Enlightenment, the bourgeois honesty of the citizens and of the merchants became blurred (see Burkhart 2006: 93). The kind of honourability remained relatively stable in this respect and passed to the bourgeoisie and the bourgeois merchants (see Sombart, 1920). Sombart has described the bourgeois Honourable Merchants in detail (see Chapter 137, 160–163, chapter 12, with a focus on the relationship to the community). He identifies the bourgeois economic rules, such as the principle of keeping the revenue larger than the ex-

penditures (ibid.: 137–139). In addition, economic arguments about ethical behaviour increasingly defined the relationship between merchants and the outside world (ibid., 160) where the litmus test for economic activities and their ethical justification became "commercial soundness"; i.e. the reliability in keeping promises, 'real' service and the accuracy in meeting obligations. For Sombart, this is the 'morality of the treaty,' since the relations among merchants were not necessarily personal, but were rules-based and related to the business as an organisation. The morality of the treaty as a virtue contains the principles of simplicity, truthfulness, loyalty, and honesty (ibid., 161). In Europe, these principles had to internalise every person who wanted to become a merchant until the eighteenth century (cf. ibid.: 162).

In England, the *The Complete English Tradesman* was a widely used guide since the early 18th Century (Defoe 1839), with the French equivalent, the *Le Parfait Négociant* (1675) by Jacques Savary predating it and serving as a basis. In the balance between business and the well-being of the community, it was very important for bourgeois merchants to recognise that seeing only their own advantage was ethically wrong (see Sombart 1920: 207). "To supply good and genuine goods" (ibid.) was self-evident. The image of early-time Honourable Merchants reveals the consistent continuation of the ideals of the ancient and middle-aged Honourable Merchants just before the dawn of modernity.

As the early modern age evolved into the industrial era, there were many efforts by entrepreneurs (they often called themselves merchants) to preserve or even develop the image of the Honourable Merchants. One of them was Oswald Bauer. His *The Honourable Merchant and His Reputation*, based on personal experience (Bauer, 1906), marks a milestone, as it deals in depth with everyday commercial life of its time and explicitly illuminates how commercial activity should be carried out honestly and honourably. Analysing and structuring the text, the core structure of the Honourable Merchant, who had to have general, specialised knowledge, and advanced training, would be able to demonstrate the necessary skills that are essential for economic success. This 'proficient merchant' becomes Honourable if he (still most likely to be male than female. There were no female merchants of note in recorded history before the 20th century) is also of good character and good manners, which also enable him to think in the long term (cf. ibid: 135). Bauer, thus, already addressed aspects of sustainability in commercial activity more than a hundred years ago. The epochal change of industrialisation, which defines the entrepreneur as the dominant economic subject, is also reflected in Bauer's Honourable Merchants, who behave honestly towards employees, customers, suppliers and competitors. Towards the end of his book, which considers international trade in detail, Bauer focuses on the relationship of the merchants to "his" community, suggesting that merchants should feel obliged to support the common good, which reflects ancient political positions, and are continuations of the activity of bourgeois Honourable Merchants. Through his work,

Bauer creates perspectives which are transformed into a management science theory that was still in its infancy, but which also involved an awareness of the respectable commercial behaviour.

7. | Corporate Purpose and Responsibility of Honourable Merchants

The historical analysis has shown that the ideal of Honourable Merchants with their ancient predecessors has hardly changed since the Middle Ages and overlaps with the more legalistic and philosophical tradition that began with Adam Smith and became codified in legal doctrine in the 20th century. The guiding principle has always been part of the training of merchants and consciously educated. The socio-historical analysis shows that society at any time determines by and large what is "honourable" for merchants, or more contemporary, what is "responsible". The responsibility model Honourable Merchant rests on three pillars (see Figure 1): self-responsibility, corporate responsibility and responsibility towards the economy and society.

7-1. Self-Responsibility

The basis for self-responsibility is humanistic. On this basis, Honourable Merchants need a comprehensive economic expertise and a solid character, oriented towards virtues that promote economic efficiency. The virtues do not serve primarily to accomplish good deeds, they serve their own credibility, which creates trust, which in turn is essential for good business relations. The sound character also protects the merchant from ill-considered acts,

Figure 1   Responsibility Model Honourable Merchant

Self-Responsibility	Corporate Responsibility	Responsibility for Economy & Society
· Orientation on merchants virtues · Cosmopolitan and liberal · Stands by his word · Business judgment	· Role model of his activities · Provides prerequisites for honourable behavior · Long-term and sustainable activities	· Principal of good faith · Takes responsibility within society · Pursues values also in international businesses

source: own representation

for example, of obtaining other advantages at short notice. For Honourable Merchants, business and ethics can not be separated from one another, they have merged into a unity with the aim of successfully managing its business as a way of discharging the individual's duty. Honourable Merchants develop a sense of responsibility for the things that determine their business success.

7-2. Corporate Responsibility

The sense of responsibility of Honourable Merchants at the company level is characterised by their relationship with their employees. The satisfaction of the employees causes, and not just contributes to, commercial success. Employees are to be treated fair and humane but are also expected to perform. Secondly, business customers and their suppliers follow which Honourable Merchants apply their principles with the aim of establishing and maintaining good relations with them in the long term. Personal ties strengthen the company, and this extends to relations with investors who should place long-term trust in the company.

7-3. Responsibility Towards Business and Society

The responsibility does not end at the factory gate. Honourable Merchants know that the society in which they run their company is decisive for the success of the company. However, members of society are not always aware that they can only prosper when an economy creates and promotes responsible entrepreneurship. On the part of business, however, the basic understanding is more likely to be that companies and society are dependent on one another if they want to increase their respective prosperity.

To this extent, Honourable Merchants have a strong sense of responsibility regarding the corporate as well as the society level. The latter can be seen, for example, by social engagement at the company's location, public and political information about the company's activities and objectives, the defence of the market economy, and sustainable environmental protection in all company decisions.

8. | Conclusion

Especially since the financial market crisis, the call for responsible corporate management has become louder. Citizens in many countries fear that existing control mechanisms might not be enough to put a stop to financial gamblers in an ethics-void context in the future. To this extent, the financial crisis revealed both societal and corporate deficiencies in the basic understanding of responsible, sustainable, honourable and thus successful, corporate leadership.

Most of the public is likely to agree that only those who are economically successful are also able to act efficiently in the interest of society and the environment. And this in turn means that the economic viability of companies and the willingness to assume responsible management are inseparable.

At this point, Corporate Purpose and the principles of Honourable Merchants coincide and come into play. As has been shown, the guiding principles assume that responsible behaviour enacted by those in leadership position is the basis for sustainable economic success and social peace in society. While much of this had been lost as social responsibility became more codified in law rather than driven by practice and collective value, today we may be seeing a move back from legal doctrine to moral suasion and collective value based action.

Modern Honourable Merchants have a strong sense of responsibility on the corporate as well as the societal level. This includes fair behaviour towards employees, customers and business partners, as well as the development and supply of innovative products and services, social commitment at the company's location, transparency of company's policy towards the public, defence of the market economy, and sustainable environmental protection in all company decisions.

In this context, it is encouraging to see that most of companies have long recognised the benefits of sustainable business and have included responsibility into their corporate strategy. In this respect one cannot transfer the misconduct of a few to judge all managers or even all entrepreneurs. After all, not every (financial) manager exercises short-term interests to the expense of the long-term and sustainable economic success, namely the traditional entrepreneurial principle of Honourable Merchants.

It should also be noted that frequent controls by auditors and regulatory authorities, of the supervisory boards, as well as the greed of small and large investors, have made possible higher returns while neglecting business risks. The recent financial market crisis certainly had numerous causes. But, as the argument above has shown the misconduct of their actors was primarily individual and not institutional, and many examples of "dishonourable" merchants and their criticism by society exist throughout history as well.

Arguably, economic crises create opportunities to learn and to stimulate a discourse on the relationship between business and society.

Economy and society are mutually and inter-dependent with companies prospering mainly in modern societies with a high level of education for their citizens, well functioning markets and strong legal certainty. On the other hand, modern societies depend on successful companies, as only these can increase the prosperity of a society through market success. Companies and society are therefore interdependent and the value systems that guide both are mutually reinforcing.

Responsible leadership based on the guiding principles of Honourable Merchants will continue to be the success formula to ensure economic and social progress in the long-term.

〈References〉

Aristoteles (2005) *Die Nikomachische Ethik*, Düsseldorf: Artemis & Winkler.

Baloglou, C. P. and Constantinides, A. (1993) *Die Wirtschaft in der Gedankenwelt der alten Griechen*, Bern: Peter Lang.

—— and Peukert, H. (1996) *Zum antiken ökonomischen Denken der Griechen (800–31 v.u.Z.) – Eine kommentierte Bibliographie*, 2nd edition. Marburg: Metropolis-Verlag.

Bauer, O. (1906) *Der ehrbare Kaufmann und sein Ansehen*, Dresden: Steinkopff und Springer.

Burkhart, D. (2006) Eine Geschichte der Ehre, Darmstadt: Wissenschaftlicher Buchverlag.

DCGK (2017) German Corporate Governance Code.

Defoe, D. (1839) *The Complete English Tradesman*, Originally published in 1726, now reprinted with notes, Edinburgh: William and Robert Chambers.

Devinney, T. M., Williams, C. A. and Schwalbach, J. (eds.) (2013) Corporate Social Responsibility and Corporate Governance: Comparative Perspectives, *Corporate Governance: An International Review*, Volume 21, Issue 5, pp. 413–419.

Dotson, J. (2002) Fourteenth Century Merchant Manuals and Merchant Culture, in M. A. Denzel, C. J. Hocquet, & H. Witthöft (eds.), *Kaufmannsbücher und Handelspraktiken vom Spätmittelalter bis zum beginnenden 20. Jahrhundert*, Stuttgart: Franz Steiner Verlag: pp. 75–87.

Driftmann, H. H. (2010) Das Leitbild des Ehrbaren Kaufmanns revitalisieren, in: DIHK (eds.), *Ehrensache – Engagiert für die Gesellschaft*, Berlin: DIHK: pp. 5–7.

Fellmeth, U. (2008) *Pecunia non olet – die Wirtschaft der antiken Welt*, Darmstadt: Wissenschaftliche Buchgesellschaft.

Freeman, R. E. (1984) *Strategic Management: A Stakeholder Approach*, Pitman Series in Business and Public Policy.

Le Goff, J. (1993) *Kaufleute und Bankiers im Mittelalter*, Frankfurt am Main: Campus Verlag.

Leibinger, B. (2006) Der Ehrbare Kaufmann – Auslaufmodell oder Leitbild in einer globalen Wirtschaft, Vortrag Humboldt-Universität zu Berlin, 27. Oktober 2006.

Pacioli, L. (1494) *Summa de arithmetica geometrica proportioni et proportionalità*, Vinegia: Paganino de Paganini.

Rumelt, R. P. (2012) *Good Strategy/Bad Strategy: The Difference and Why it Matters*, Strategic Direction, Vol. 28, No. 8.

Savary, J. (1697) *Le Parfait Négociant*, Jac Lyon.

Simon, H. (1992) *Lessons from Germany's Midsize Giants*, Harvard Business Review, March-April, pp. 116–123.

Smith, A. (1759) *Theory of Moral Sentiments*, London.

Sombart, W. (1920) *Der Bourgeois – Zur Geistesgeschichte des modernen Wirtschaftsmenschen*, München: Duncker und Humblot.

Sommer, A. Jr. (1991) Whom Should the Corporation Serve? The Berle-Dodd Debate Revisited Sixty Years Later, *Delaware Journal of Corporate Law*, Vol. 16, No. 1.

14　企業と社会フォーラム学会誌，第 10 号，pp. 14-30，2021

日本におけるポストコロナと
持続可能な「企業と社会」

関正雄（損害保険ジャパン株式会社）

今津秀紀（凸版印刷株式会社）

黒田かをり（一般財団法人 CSO ネットワーク）

福川恭子（一橋大学大学院経営管理研究科教授）

岡本大輔（慶應義塾大学商学部教授）

司会　谷本寛治（早稲田大学商学学術院商学部教授）

（本稿は，2021 年 3 月 6 日にオンラインで開催された JFBS シンポジウム「日本におけるポストコロナと持続可能な『企業と社会』」をまとめたものである。）

1. ｜ イントロダクション

谷本　寛治

JFBS は本日のシンポジウムに先立ち，2021 年 1 月 23 日に国際シンポジウム "Sustainability Management in Post-Corona Era" をオンラインで開催した。アジア（韓国・中国，タイ，インドネシア，台湾）とロシアからスピーカーに集まっていただき，ポストコロナにおけるサステナビリティ経営にかかわる課題についてグローバルな視点から議論を行った。（Dr. Jung Wan Lee ／ Professor, School of International Economics and Trade, Anhui University of Finance and Economics, Dr. Maxim Storchevoy ／ Associate Professor, HSE University, Director of Russian Business Ethics Network, Dr. Daniel McFarlane ／ Director of MA in Social Innovation & Sustainability, School of Global Studies, Thammasat University, Dr. Juniati Gunawan ／ Director of Trisakti Sustainability Center, Trisakti University, Dr. Niven Huang ／ Regional Leader of KPMG Sustainability Services in Asia Pacific, KPMG Sustainability Consulting）。

そこでは各国のコロナ禍における経済，企業経営にかかわる現状，課題，支援策から，労働，環境，貧困問題への対応やデジタル化の新たな可能性，ESG 投資・グリーン金融の重要性が指摘された。

＊このシンポジウムについては，JFBS 事務局が取りまとめた梗概が，『オルタナ』さらに『Yahoo！ニュース』（3/3）に「環境・倫理・デジタル化，ポストコロナの企業経営」のタイトルで掲載されているので参照されたい。

本日のシンポジウムでは日本に焦点を当て，

ポストコロナと持続可能な「企業と社会」を
テーマに，サステナビリティの課題，持続可能
な企業と社会のあり方について議論を行う。コ
ロナ禍によって経済・社会が混乱，低迷してい
る中，今後，持続可能な社会経済システムをど
のように構築していけば良いのか。HSBC の調
査によると，これまで CSR ／サステナビリ
ティ・マネジメントへの対応，ステイクホル
ダー・エンゲージメント，リスク対応を地道に
行ってきた企業とそうでない企業とでは，コロ
ナ禍への対応力，レジリエンスにも差がみられ
る，と指摘されている。ニューノーマル（新常
態）では，システムの変革と継続がみられる
が，ポストコロナにおいて，何が問い直され，
どのように対応していけば良いのか，多様な視
点から議論する。

　現在は VUCA の時代という言い方がなされ
ている。VUCA とは，Volatility：不安定さ，
Uncertainty：不確実さ，Complexity：複雑さ，
Ambiguity：曖昧さの頭文字を取った言葉で，
とても厄介な時代に今私たちはいると言える。
もうひとつ，Black Elephant という言い方が
なされている。Black Swan は，ご存知の通
り，白鳥の中にまれに黒鳥が現れる，めったに
起きないこと，期待していない出来事の中から
予期しない結果が出てくる，ということ。Ele-
phant in the room という言葉も以前よりあ
り，これは大きな象が部屋の中にいて，邪魔な
のだけれど，悪さをしなければ見て見ぬふりを
しているのだが，いったん問題が起きたら大変
なことになってしまう。この 2 つの言葉からつ
くられたのが Black Elephant。つまり，地球
温暖化，自然災害，そして今回のコロナのよう
な感染症は人類の長い歴史の中で何度も危機的
な状況を引き起こしてきた。Black Elephant
は，近々起こるリスクがわかっているけれど
も，なかなか対応がなされていない，でも起き

てしまうと大変な問題になってしまうことを示
している。

　ところでコロナ以前から議論されてきた経
済，環境，社会に関わる持続可能な社会のあり
方，企業の CSR，サステナビリティ経営など
の課題には，さまざまな取り組みがなされてき
た。コロナ後においては新たな課題のみなら
ず，これまで議論されてきたことが待ったなし
で対応を迫られている。例えば，産業構造の転
換，働き方，雇用のスタイル，移民・労働力不
足，消費行動の変化，コミュニケーションスタ
イルの変化，デジタルトランスフォーメーショ
ンの進展，さらには不平等，教育の問題など。

　プラットフォーム・ビジネスのようにコロナ
禍で大きく成長している分野もあれば，交通，
観光，飲食など非常に厳しく先の見えない状況
の産業もあり，大きな開きがみられる。さらに
景気回復は製造業と非製造業で二極化し，「K
字型」との指摘もなされている。

　働き方については，リモートワークが以前か
ら言われてきたが，日本ではなかなか定着せ
ず，それに対応した仕組みもできてこなかっ
た。IT 基盤の問題だけではなく，そもそもの
仕事の仕方，評価の仕方にかかわる問題であ
る。

　いわゆる雇い止めによる失業，非正規労働
者，外国人労働者の問題。さらにグローバルに
は移民労働者が入ってこないという状況で，人
手不足となる状況があり，ポストコロナになる
とこれが労働力の奪い合いになるのではないか
と言われている。

　消費者が自宅でさまざまなプラットフォーム
のサービスを利用し，巣ごもりで需要が増える
ことで，消費者行動が変わってきている。また
そこにはごみの増加や人づきあいの減少という
ネガティブな問題も出ている。

　コロナ禍において改めてコミュニケーション

のあり方，働き方，仕事の仕方，ビジネスのスタイルが問い直されているが（教育の問題も），そのベースとなるデジタル社会への対応（DX）の遅れが指摘されている。さまざまな課題に取り組むに当たって，関係するステイクホルダーが協働していくことが，今回のコロナ禍の中で問われている。

本日は次の5名の方々（JFBSのメンバー）をスピーカーとしてお招きした。まず，損害保険ジャパン，明治大学でも特任教授をされている関正雄氏。ポストコロナと企業の役割についてお話しいただく。

二番目に，凸版印刷の今津秀紀氏。同社ではSDGsに関わるさまざまな取り組みがされており，新しいケースを見ながら，メーカー側，消費者側，両方からの動きについて紹介していただく。

三番目はNGOの代表として黒田かをり氏。CSOネットワークでは，SDGsの課題についてさまざまな発言をされているが，今回はコロナ禍における社会的な課題に焦点を当て，多様でインクルーシブな社会の実現に向けてお話しいただく。

四番目は，一橋大学大学院経営管理研究科の福川恭子教授。マーケティングやビジネスエシックスの専門家の視点から，コロナ禍で変化した消費者行動のポジティブ／ネガティブな面を考え，それは今後変わっていくことのスタートとなるのか，考えていただく。

最後は，慶應義塾大学商学部の岡本大輔教授。これまでのCSRのパフォーマンス，CSP（Corporate Social Performance）とFinancial Performanceに関する研究に基づき，ポストコロナでの企業評価についてお話しいただく。

まずそれぞれのお話をしていただき，その後質問も受けつつ議論を進めていきたいと思う。

2. ポストコロナと企業の役割

関　正雄

ポストコロナと企業の役割について考えるうえで，まず新型コロナとSDGs（国連持続可能な開発目標）との関係を考えてみたい。世界を襲ったコロナ禍は，社会に甚大な悪影響をもたらしている。人々の健康はもちろん，経済，雇用など多く指標が悪化し，SDGsの達成にとっては明らかにマイナスである。また，相対的により大きな影響を受けたのは社会の中で弱い立場に置かれた人々である。まさに，コロナ禍は社会の脆弱性と問題点をあぶりだしたと言えよう。こうした危機に直面して，コロナ対応でSDGsどころではない，と考えてしまいがちだが，真実は逆で，「誰も取り残さない」というSDGsの理念の実現に向けて，取り組みをますます加速する必要がある。

また，コロナ禍においてSDGsのウェディングケーキの図の意味するところが腑に落ちたように思う（図1）。経済は社会を土台として営まれるもので，まず感染を抑え込まない限り経済は元に戻らないことを私たちは痛感させられた。この図を頭で理解するだけではなく実感を伴って理解したのは，コロナ禍に直面したからとも言えよう。

ポストコロナにおいてめざすべきは，「よりよい再建」である。そしてキーワードは，脱炭素社会への移行をテコにした「グリーン・リカバリー」であり，より「強靭」で「包摂的な」社会の実現である。SDGs達成に中心的な役割を期待されている企業セクターも，ポストコロナにおけるSDGsへの取り組みの重要性を最認識して，さらに積極的に行動すべきである。

図1　SDGs のウェディングケーキ

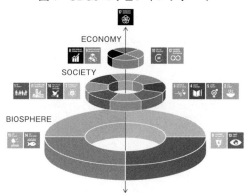

出典：Azote Images for Stockholm Resilience Centre, Stockholm University

2-1. 変わる日本産業界

経団連は，2017 年に企業行動憲章を大幅に改定し，世界共通目標となった SDGs，グローバル行動規範としての国連「ビジネスと人権に関する指導原則」などを組み込んだ。その前文では，企業は「持続可能な社会の実現をけん引する」存在であると位置付けて，会員企業に SDGs を事業戦略に組み込むように促している。

その後，会員企業は確かに変化している。2020 年 10 月に発表された調査結果[1]では，2 年前と比べて SDGs をビジネス戦略に組み込んでいる企業は 10％から 42％へと大幅に増加した。

また経団連では，こうした動きを加速するために，2020 年 3 月に「ESG 投資の進化，Society 5.0 の実現，そして SDGs の達成へ」と題した，東京大学・GPIF（年金積立金管理運用独立行政法人）との共同研究会の報告書を発表した。さらに注目すべきは，コロナ禍のさなかである 2020 年 11 月に経団連が発表した「。新成長戦略」である。この表題の句点「。」は，SDGs に必要とされるトランスフォーメーションを実現するために，これまでの路線に一旦終止符「。」を打って，サステナブルな資本主義を実現するという意思の表明である。その戦略

のなかで，格差の是正，バックキャスティング，マルチステイクホルダー，といった SDGs におけるキーワードに言及している。描かれたポストコロナの新成長戦略は，社会において果たすべき企業の役割をより強く意識した，SDGs の理念に立脚したものである，と言えよう。

2-2. 取り組みが遅れるビジネスと人権

ポストコロナの時代において取り組みを強化すべき重要な課題のひとつは，人権である。

日本政府は 2020 年 10 月に，「ビジネスと人権に関する行動計画」を取りまとめた。国連「ビジネスと人権に関する指導原則」を踏まえて策定したもので，企業に対しては，企業活動における人権リスクの特定，予防，救済，情報公開を行う，すなわち人権デューディリジェンス導入への期待が表明されている。

経団連のアンケート調査によると，先述のように会員企業の SDGs の経営への統合が大きく進展している半面，人権に関する取り組みは残念ながら進んでいない。2018 年と 2020 年との比較で，人権デューディリジェンスへ取り組む企業の割合はいずれも約 30％と変化していない。

ポストコロナの時代にめざすべき人間中心の包摂的な社会の実現において，人権はその根底になければならず，精神論ではなく具体的なマネジメントの対象課題として経営にビルトインすることが求められる。この点は日本企業の課題として強調しておきたい。

2-3. 関心を高めるべき生物多様性

もうひとつの課題は，生物多様性である。気候変動は企業戦略への組み込みが進んでいるが，生物多様性は，きわめて重要な課題であるにも関わらず，取り組む企業ははるかに少な

い。気候変動に比べて取り上げられる機会が少なく問題意識を持ちにくいかもしれないが，経済や社会の土台である生態系が危機に瀕しておりその保全自体が重要であるだけではなく，気候変動の緩和と適応の両面でその解決に資するテーマでもある。2021 年に中国で開催予定の生物多様性条約の COP15 では，気候変動におけるパリ協定に匹敵する重要なグローバル枠組みが論議される。こうした議論に日本企業も参加するとともに，自社の戦略を描いていくべきであろう。グローバルには，政策決定に関与すべく BFN（Business for Nature）というイニシアチブがスタートしているし，また気候変動における TCFD と同様の，経営戦略と一体化した情報開示の新たな枠組み（TNFD: Task Force on Nature-related Financial Disclosure）策定の構想が立ち上がっている。国内外ステイクホルダーからの企業への取り組み要請は，ますます強まるであろう。

2-4. 長期的思考力を鍛えること

　最後に，ポストコロナの時代に求められる，長期的思考力について述べておきたい。SDGs の浸透で 2030 年がマイルストーンイヤーとして認識されるようになったが，それは文字通り一つの通過点でしかない。その先にめざす社会像への想像力と，長期的なビジョンを自身の戦略や行動に落とし込む構想力を鍛える必要がある。

　その意味で注目すべきレポートが，2021 年 3 月に発表された WBCSD の Vision 2050（Refresh）である。2050 年を展望したビジネス界からのこの提言レポートは，もともと 2010 年に発表されたものである。超長期のグローバルな変化を見据えて，90 億人が地球上でまともな暮らしができる（Nine billion people can live well, within the limits of the Planet.）ために何を

しなければならないかを検討し，ステイクホルダーへの問題提起と企業自らのアクション強化を説いた。WBCSD の会員企業 40 社が議論を重ね，これを 10 年ぶりに刷新したものが，今回の提言レポートである。今回のレポートの副題は Time to transform であり，systems transformation，すなわち長期的視点に立って問題の根本原因まで掘り下げたうえで大変革を成し遂げること，そのためのステイクホルダーとのエンゲージメントが重要であることを強調している。

　2010 年に初版が発表された頃に比べて，日本企業の視野は大きく広がり，SDGs や 2030 年をにらんだ長期戦略を描く企業の数も増えてきた。しかし，今後さらにその先までを視野に入れることが，SDGs への取り組み強化のためにも必要である。

3. | 凸版印刷のサステナビリティ経営 － TOPPAN Business Action for SDGs の発表と実行

今津　秀紀

3-1. 2 段階の SDGs STATEMENT 発表

　凸版印刷株式会社（以下，トッパン）のサステナビリティ経営について紹介する。現在のトッパンは SDGs 達成への貢献に力を注いでおり，2019 年と 2020 年に 2 段階の SDGs STATEMENT を発表した。

　1 回目の SDGs STATEMENT では取り組むべきマテリアリティを特定した。全社活動（トッパン自体の活動）と事業活動（ビジネスを通じて社会的課題に挑戦する活動）に整理して，SDGs 宣言を社内外に発表した。

　2 回目は TOPPAN Business Action for SDGs である。Business Action と示す通り，

社会にポジティブインパクトを生み出すビジネスを推進する宣言である。

3-2. サーキュラーエコノミーの実現に向けたトッパンのビジネス事例紹介

TOPPAN Business Action for SDGs で設定した目標の中の1つ「サーキュラーエコノミーの実現」についてビジネス事例を紹介する。

理想とするのは新たな石油資源などを使わずに，今ある資源だけで循環する社会。廃棄物をなくし，生産時も使用時も CO_2 を限りなく減らす。もちろんそこにはすべての人々が安心して心豊かに暮らせる社会という理想がある。

しかしながら，一足飛びにサーキュラーエコノミーへ移行することは難しい。そこで，企業各社がスタートさせたのが，原材料を可能な限り減らす設計，脱プラに向けた素材開発や置き換え，リサイクルがしやすいように複合材からモノ素材への設計変更である。つまり資源循環のシステムに乗せるための各パーツづくりが始まったと言える。トッパンもさまざまなアプローチを行っているが，その中から取り組みを2例紹介する。

1つ目が「カートカン」である。紙製の缶飲料。国産材や間伐材を使用しており，さらには当社開発の GL フィルムや充填の工夫から一般の箱型紙製飲料と比較して1.5〜2倍の長期保存が可能になる。使用後には牛乳パックと同様にリサイクルができる。間伐材の利用や技術開発に加えて，既存の回収システムに乗せられるように設計することで資源循環を目指す。

2つ目が「エコクラシー」である。オリンピックなどの大規模スポーツイベント会場をイメージしてほしい。横断幕などの装飾メディアが会場内外に数多く飾られている。従来のものは複数の素材が混ざっているためにリサイクルには適さず最終的には埋め立て処分されてい

た。そこで，使用後に別の製品へと生まれ変わることができるマテリアルリサイクル設計を行い，会場跡地の公園ベンチや他用途に使えるようにした。今後は国際的なスポーツイベントや大規模な展示会場へ採用されることを期待している。イベント会場に集中するからこそ，終了後には回収しやすいという実現可能性から生まれた（図2）。

3-3. TOPPAN SDGs Unit キックオフ

資源循環への取り組みが当社ビジネスに対する次のヒントもくれた。サステナビリティやSDGs は決して単発の取り組みではなく言葉の通りに持続的でなければならない。あるビジネスの好影響が違うところでは悪影響を与えるようなトレードオフの関係になってはならない。

そこで，パーパスや目標策定などのアドバイス業務→さまざまな素材，包材，プロモーション，DX などを支援する業務→ PR や情報発信などのコミュニケーション業務まで SDGs バリューチェーン全体を広く捉えて支援していくTOPPAN SDGs Unit を立ち上げた。本 Unitでは SDGs ウォッシュにならないようにチェック機能も受け持つ（図3）。

3-4. アドバイザリー業務からみるポストコロナ3つの影響

最後に前項で紹介した TOPPAN SDGs Unitの中で，パーパスや目標策定に関わる仕事をしている立場からポストコロナに向けてどのような変化がみられるかを3点紹介する。

・DX と人材育成―DX の加速によりマテリアリティの特定で人材育成の重要度が高まった。そして，リモートワークの広がりが社員の働き方も変えることから心の健康に注目する企業も増加している。

・SDGs と ESG 投資―定量目標の設定と中期

図2　カートカン　エコクラシー

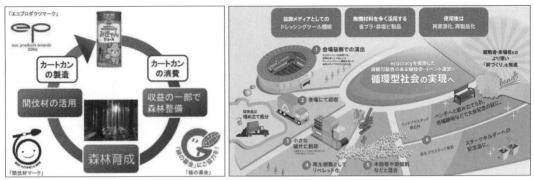

図3　TOPPAN SDGs Unit

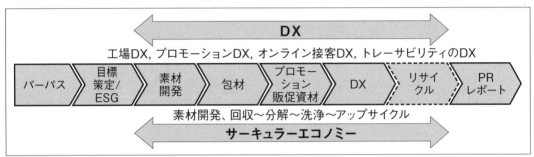

経営計画への組み込みも大手企業を中心に広がっている。ESG 投資成長の影響も大きい。投資家は 2030 年にどこまでやるのか，今はどこまでできているのか，中計の最終年はどこまで目指すのかを判断材料にするからである。

・サプライチェーンの取り組み―従来の人権・労働問題に加えて，環境（スコープ 3）がクローズアップされ始めた。CO_2 ネットゼロを目指すにはバリューチェーン全体で取り組む必要がある。再びサプライチェーンに対する要請が高まってきそうだ。

4. アフターコロナ：多様でインクルーシブな社会の実現を

黒田　かをり

新型コロナウィルスの感染拡大は，世界中で経済，雇用，社会，福祉等に大きな打撃を与えている。とりわけ，社会で取り残されるリスクの高い人たちへの影響は深刻である。日本において取り残されがちな人々とは，NPO 法人「人間の安全保障」フォーラムによると，「子ども，女性，若者，高齢者，障害者，LGBT 等の性的マイノリティ，災害被害者，外国人」等である[2]。なお，持続可能な開発目標（SDGs）は，「誰一人取り残されない」持続可能な社会の実現を最上位目標としている。雇用等に関して，具体的にどのような影響が出ているのかについて，いくつか公表されている調査結果とデータを見てみる。

新型コロナウィルスが働く女性に与える影響に関して実施された『新型コロナウイルスと雇用・暮らしに関する NHK・JILPT 共同調査[3]』によれば，雇用に変化が起きたと回答した人は，男性が回答者の 18.7％ であるのに対し，女

性は 26.3％であった。特に非正規労働者の女性は回答者の 33.1％が雇用に変化があったと答えている。また同調査では，収入が 3 割以上減少した人の割合について，非正規の女性が 26.1％，シングルマザーが 24.6％と高い数字を表している。

　プライドハウス東京コンソーシアムは，新型コロナウィルスが LGBTQ 等性的マイノリティのユースに与えた影響について緊急オンライン調査を実施した[4]。その結果を見ると，回答者の 25％が失業・休職／休業を経験しており，収入が減少する見込みと答えた人は 38.5％に上っている。また回答者の 4 割弱がコロナ禍で安心できる人や場所との繋がりが脆弱になったと答えている。

　障害者の雇用状況も悪化している。厚生労働省の調査結果[5]によると，企業の業績悪化等を理由に解雇された障害者は，2020 年 4 月から 9 月までの半年間で 1,213 人に上り，前年の同時期に比べて 342 人，約 40％増えた。その中でも知的障害者は前年より 80％増加した。その理由として新型コロナウィルスの感染拡大でテレワークが広がり職場への出社が必要な事務職等の仕事が減っており，障害者が働くことができる新たな仕事の創出が課題，と分析されている。

　さらに深刻な影響を受けているのが日本にいる外国人である。情報がない，住居がない，身分がない，食べ物がないという状態で，技能実習失踪者，飲食店等コロナの打撃を受けた業種で働く留学生や難民申請者等が最も深刻な影響を受けている[6]。

4-1.　持続可能でインクルーシブな社会に向けた NPO 等の実践

　このような状況において，民間非営利組織（NPO）は，パンデミックや災害で被害を大き

く受ける人々やグループを直接支援する役割を担っている。NPO の具体的な実践は，住まいや収入を失った人への支援，日本に住む外国人への支援，障害者への生活・就労支援，困窮する世帯や生徒／学生への奨学金等の給付等多岐にわたる。

　また NPO の呼びかけに応じて緊急支援を行う人々も増加している。NPO 法人自立生活サポートセンター・もやい（以下，「もやい」）は「住まいや収入を失った人を支援したい！」というクラウドファンディングをコロナの感染拡大の第 1 波を迎えた 2020 年春（3 月 29 日～4 月 30 日）と年末年始に向けた冬（12 月 1 日～2021 年 1 月 15 日）に 2 回実施した[7]。支援総額は春が 10,959,000 円，冬が 9,161,836 円で「もやい」が当初目標額とした 100 万円を優に超えている。

　また，移住者と連帯する全国ネットワークは，「新型コロナ『移民・難民緊急支援』」を 2020 年 5 月に立ち上げ，9 月 14 日時点で寄付総額と助成総額を合わせて 49,794,564 円を集めた[8]。

　持続可能でインクルーシブな社会の実現に向けた取り組みとして福島県郡山市にある NPO 法人しんせい（以下，しんせい）の農福連携を取り上げたい。しんせいは 10 年前の東日本大震災発生後の福島第一原子力発電所の事故で福島県中通り等に避難してきた障害者福祉事業所の立て直しやそれぞれの利用者たちの生活再建の手伝いをしながら，「誇りある仕事づくり」を始めた。その後，NPO や企業の支援を受けて 12 の事業所と協働プロジェクトを開始，企業の技術指導や寄付を受け，利用者一人ひとりに合わせた仕事づくりを大事にしながら，焼き菓子やデニムバック等を販売している。しんせいの事業は，多様なステイクホルダーとの連携が鍵となっている。連携相手には，地方自治

体，企業，労働組合，NPO といった組織から，農家，地元の人たち，ボランティア等個人もたくさんいる。

しかしコロナの感染拡大でマルシェ等やイベントがなくなり，売り上げが落ち込んでしまった。コロナ前から郡山市逢瀬町に農業法人との協働で遊休地を活用した農福連携事業を計画していたが，コロナをきっかけにオンラインでアイディア出し等事業に関わったり，時には現地に行き加工場づくりに参加したりする都会の人たちが増えた。また再生可能エネルギーの導入も専門家や関係者を交えて具体的に検討が始まっており，まさに持続可能でインクルーシブな場づくりを実践している（図4）。

4-2. 新型コロナウィルスを「変革」のきっかけに

アフターコロナの社会を考える際に，以前の生活に戻すのではなく，Build Back Better（より良い復興），つまり前よりも良い状態にすることが期待される。2030 年を期限として国際社会が達成を目指している SDGs は，「我々の世界を変革する（transforming）―持続可能な開発のための 2030 アジェンダ」であり，持続可能かつインクルーシブ（社会包摂）な社会の実現が求められている。つまりこれまでの延長ではなくこの社会を抜本的に見直す「変革」が必要とされている。新型コロナウィルスの感染拡大というこの未曾有の事態を「変革」のきっかけにすることが大事である。

5. コロナ禍で変化した消費者行

福川　恭子

近年，企業努力が注がれている持続可能な開発目標達成（SDGs）には，企業・消費者行動

図4 「山の農園」の加工場

出所：写真は特定非営利活動法人しんせい提供。

の抜本的な変化が必要とされている。Sheth（2020）[9] によると，消費者行動は次の 4 つの要因によって変化する。1 つ目は結婚，出産，引っ越しなど人生周期に経験する「ライフイベント」による変化。2 つ目は固定電話から携帯電話，インターネットなどにみられる「新しいテクノロジー」に適応する変化。3 つ目は受動喫煙対策などにみられる「公的または共有スペースに関わる規則・規制・統制」に順応する変化，4 つ目は，当シンポジウムのテーマであるコロナ感染拡大などにみられる，「予期することの難しい災害」によって行動変化である。コロナ禍で変化した消費者行動は次の 8 つエリアである（Sheth, 2020）。

1) Hoarding：買いだめ。感染拡大による不要不急外出規制が始まった頃，トイレットペーパーやマスク，食料品などの買いだめ現象。将来的不透明さや，供給不足からインフレーションなどへの心配から起こる。

2) Improvisation：即興・間に合わせと呼ばれる行動。感染拡大により手に入らない商品や現実不可能なサービスを，何らかの工夫を施して代替，満足すること。企

業・消費者の工夫とクリエーティビティーで乗り越える消費場面を指し，ズーム越しの葬式や結婚式，オンラインや電話越しの診察サービス，オンライン教育などが例として挙げられる。

3) Pent-up demand：災害や不透明な状況下で延期されている消費をさす繰越需要。車，家，電化製品など比較的高価な商品の購入控を一般例として挙げられるが，コロナ禍でサーキュレーターや体温計測器など特殊な電化製品は，逆に需要が増えている。コロナ禍で，繰越されている需要で顕著なものは，感染防止のために密を避けるために，コンサート，スポーツ観戦，観光，外食が挙げられる。

4) Embracing Digital Technology：デジタル技術を取り入れた消費形態。必要に迫られて，デジタル技術を取り入れ商品やサービス消費場面が増加。先に上げられたオンライン診療，オンライン教育や急増したデジタル決済などが事例に当たる。ビデオ機能のあるアプリで定期的なオンライン交流も増加。Facebook, YouTube, LINE など SNS の利用増加により，国境を越えた情報共有，クチコミの形態にも大きく影響を与えている。

5) Store comes home：「店が家に来る」と称した消費現象。主に海外で見られた完全な外出禁止（ロックダウン）でアクセスのなくなった食料品・生活必需品を配達・消費形態。この物流形態は，外出を自粛している多くの消費者にも好まれ，書籍や映画鑑賞などの他の商品・サービス分野でも取り入れられる。「どうしても買う前に実物を見たい」または「インターネットは使い慣れていない」という顧客層向けサービスでは，スーパーマーケットとバス会社などの提携による移動販売車サービスが例として挙げられる。

6) Blurring of work-life boundaries：仕事と生活の境界線が曖昧になったことで変化した消費者行動。仕事と私生活のバランスを保つために，限られた自宅のスペースをどう工夫するかは消費者が抱えている大きな課題で，その解決を促す商品（ヘッドフォン，間仕切り）やサービス（時間貸しシェアオフィス）が市場に増えた。

7) Reunion with Friends and Family：家族や友人と再結集。コロナ禍で，家族や友人同士が安否を気遣い，お互いに連絡を取り合うのをきっかけに，普段よりもさらに積極的に，自粛生活経験を共有する場面も増えた。コロナがなければ，連絡をとっていなかった友人たちとも，久しぶりに再び交流を始め，「こんな地元の特産送るよ」，「こんな番組が面白かった」，「オンラインレシピを一緒に作ろう」，「オンライン音楽会しよう」など，消費者同士の消費経験共有する交流が深まっている。

8) Discovering of Talent：才能の発見。何らかの形で仕事や学校から解放され，自分のための時間が増えた消費者がいろいろなことに挑戦している現象。例えば，「お味噌汁をだしから」や「パスタを原材料から作る」などの料理から，新しい楽器や言語の習得に及ぶ挑戦が例として挙げられる。そのような試みがオンラインビデオとして盛んに発信され，そこにイノベーションや商業的成功の可能性を見出すこともできる。

5-1. 持続可能な発展目標（SDGs）の達成に還元される消費者行動変化とは

確かに，コロナ禍でわれわれの行動は大きく変化した。この「予期することの難しい災害」（コロナ感染拡大）によって変化した消費者行動は，環境や社会に好影響もしくは負荷をかけているだろうか？　また，変化した行動は長期的に継続するであろうか？　環境的・社会的に好影響であるとすれば，近年求められているSDGs達成に不可欠な企業や消費者行動の変革のきっかけとなり継続を望みたいところだ。例えば，感染拡大対策で生産・商業活動の一時停止や観光客の減少により，大気および海洋汚染などが一時的に減少した。テレワークのため自宅で過ごす時間が増え，ワークライフバランスに好影響を与えた一面もある。その一方で，感染防止策も一環として，使い捨て商品の増加による環境的負荷，社会との繋がりを絶たれ精神的に病む者の増加による社会的負荷，非正規雇用者の失業または収入減少に見られる経済的負荷がある。さらに，デジタル技術応用によってさまざまなサービスがオンラインへ移行したが，そこでオンラインにアクセスが限られた脆弱層の消費者が取り残されている社会的負荷も顕著である。この機会に，SDGs達成にとって好影響をもたらした行動変化を確定し，長期的に継続（ニューノーマル）する術を考慮すべきであり，また，新しい行動様式による負荷を限りなくゼロに近づけるイノベーションに，企業（起業）人は取り掛かるべきであろう。

5-2. 展望

コロナ禍で外食や旅行の頻度は自粛傾向が続いているが（TDB-CAREE：消費者心理調査）[10]，部分的に需要が回復してきている商品群（ペット用品，教育・教養関連商品など）もある（総務省家計調査）[11]。1年以上の自粛生活で様子見

であった繰越需要（pent-up demand）に動きがあるのは確かである。同時に，コロナ禍で変化した暮らしに関わる価値観にも注視すべきだ。PWC「世界の消費者意識調査2020」[12]によると，今回の公衆衛生に関わる災害経験により，消費者の健康管理・セルフケアに関わる関心・行動は長期的に残るという。加えて，消費全般で安全性と（密を避けるために）アクセスのしやすさに消費者が価値を見出すと示唆されている。さらに，SDGsに焦点を置いたイノベーションへのアプローチとして，環境的・社会的好影響の持続，または負荷の減少に対応に対応する企業も増えるであろう。例えば，接触感染を懸念した上で使用が増えた使い捨て商品（例：マスク，プラスチック容器）は環境的負荷が即座に懸念され，少なからず再使用（布製マスク，容器持ち込みテイクアウト），再利用（リサイクル），代替資材利用（竹材，海藻など植物繊維原料で作られた商品）への転換がすでに見られる。感染拡大防止策により手に入らない商品やアクセス不可能なサービスを，消費者自らが知恵を絞り，どのような工夫を施して代替（improvisation）消費しているのかを理解すれば，イノベーションにも繋がるであろう。

6. ポストコロナの企業評価
―企業の社会性と CSP-CFP 関係

岡本　大輔

この1年のコロナ，それ以前の大震災，豪雨，リーマンショックなど，未曽有の大規模災害と経済危機に自分の人生観が変わった人も多いと聞く。自分の人生を社会のために活かしたい，という考え方をする学生，社会人も増えている。

企業にも同じことが言え，多くの機関投資家が従業員の健康と安全の最優先を求めるように

なってきた。社会課題と経済を両立しないと持続可能とは言えない。アメリカでも，ビジネスラウンドテーブルが，脱・株主第一主義を唱え，企業の目的を再定義して，従業員，顧客，地域社会などすべてのステイクホルダーを重視するようになってきている。これらの現象を，企業評価的に言えば，収益性・成長性だけでなく，社会性，ということになる。

企業評価における良い企業の条件は，高収益性・高成長性であったが，現代企業の社会的影響力を考慮すると，自分だけが儲かって伸びている企業はもはや良い企業とは言えず，高社会性を第3の企業評価基準として加えるべきと考えるからである。

この関係は以前から注目されてきたが，コロナという災害において，そしてポストコロナにおいて，以前にも増して注目され，重視されるようになっていくであろう。

社会性は現代企業にとって重要なファクターであり，収益性・成長性と並んで同じレベルの目標になっていると考えている。ただし全く同じという訳ではなく，短期的な収益性目標，中長期的な成長性目標，これに対して超長期的な社会性目標と位置づけられる。

社会性は企業に不要，という古くはフリードマンに代表されるような議論もあったが，現在では社会性の重要性は十分に認知される時代となっている。しかし，社会性が企業にとってどのような意味を持つのか，コストなのか，ベネフィットなのか，これに関してはさまざまな意見がある。CSR，サステナビリティなどの対応を地道に行ってきた企業とそうでない企業とでは，対応力，レジリエンスにも差がみられる，という指摘もある。しかし，実際にどのような差がみられるのか，という問題に関しては明確な結論は得られていない。

海外ではこれらの関係をCSP-CFP関係と呼んで，数多くの論文が発表されている。ここでは日本企業において，実際にどうなっているのか，超長期的関係が本当にみられるのかの計測を試みる。その際，社会性を「企業のさまざまなステイクホルダーに対する，自らの収益性・成長性以外のすべてのコミットメント」と定義しておく。

最初にこの計測を試みたのが1995年であった。その結果わかったことはCSPとCFPには大きな相関があり，財務業績の高い企業は社会性も高い，ということであった。この関係を詳しく見るため，4つのタイプ分けを考えた。CSPとしての社会性とCFPとしての財務業績との高低による2×2の4分類である。両者の相関が高いので，両方高いType Ⅰと両方低いType Ⅱは多いが，実際にはCFPのみ高いType ⅢもCSPのみ高いType Ⅳも存在する。

CSP-CFPの高い相関は，高業績が高社会性を呼び，それがまた高業績に繋がる好循環と，低業績が低社会性に繋がり，さらに低業績が続く悪循環を意味しているが，好循環から業績悪化への悪循環への変化と，悪循環から業績回復による好循環への変化も考えられる。

例えば，Type Ⅲ企業は，高財務業績だが，社会性は低く，社会からの要請に応えていないと考えれば，将来的には業績が悪化してしまう，とも考えられる。同様に，低財務業績企業であるType ⅡとType Ⅳを比べた場合，社会からの要請に応えていないType Ⅱより，応えているType Ⅳの方が，業績回復の可能性は高いと考えられる。

そこで，4つの仮説を立てた。社会性は高財務業績維持に貢献するという業績維持仮説，社会性は財務業績悪化を防ぐという業績悪化防止仮説，社会性の高さが財務業績回復に繋がるという業績回復仮説，社会性の高さが財務業績低迷を防ぐという業績低迷防止仮説である。これ

図5　20年後の財務業績変化

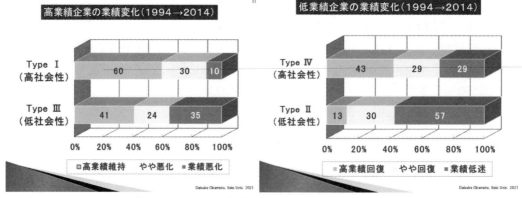

出所：詳しくは www.fbc.keio.ac.jp/~dokamoto の諸文献参照。

を5年後，10年後，そして20年後などで追跡調査を行った。

1994年に高財務業績だった Type I と Type III の20年後の業績を見ると，みごと高業績を維持した企業は，社会性の高い Type I では60％もあったが，Type III では41％だった。残念ながら低業績となってしまった企業は Type I では10％だったが，Type III では35％もあった。業績維持仮説と業績悪化防止仮説が確認できる。

低財務業績企業同士を比べると，20年後に高業績に回復した企業は社会性の高かった Type IV では43％もあったが，社会性の低かった Type II はわずか13％だった。20年後も相変わらず低迷している企業は，Type IV では29％だったが，Type II では57％も見られた。業績回復仮説と業績低迷防止仮説が確認できる（図5）。

さらに，統計的に有意な差があるかを検定してみると，最初の業績維持仮説は棄却されたが，他の3つは支持された。

社会性が高いと業績悪化を防ぐという悪化防止仮説は支持され，社会性が低いと業績悪化してしまう訳なので，社会性は高業績維持に必要と言える。

最初の業績維持仮説は，傾向としては仮説通りだったが統計的には棄却されてしまったので，高業績維持に社会性だけでは十分ではない，という結果で，当たり前と言えば当たり前と言える。

業績回復仮説は，社会性が高いと財務業績回復，低迷防止仮説は，社会性が高いと財務業績低迷防止に繋がる，ということだったので，全体として，社会性は高財務業績にとっての十分条件とは言えないが，少なくとも必要条件である，と言える。企業評価要因として，社会性を考慮することは長期的の評価において今後ますます重要になると考えられる。

最後に，25年後の2019年データの分析にも触れておく。結果は全く同じ傾向だったが，今回に限り，統計的有意性がほとんど確認できなかった。

いままで，CSP が CFP にプラスの影響を与える，ただしそれは超長期的なので，1年や2年で結果は出ない，5年，10年，20年掛かって影響が出てくる，という主張をしてきたが，それがいつまでも続くという訳ではなく，せいぜい20年くらいなのではないか，上限があるのではないか，ということを考え始めている。

一度社会性が良くなっても，それを継続する

必要は当然考えられ，今回の分析は財務データのみの追跡調査で，社会性の追跡調査を行っているわけではない。1回のCSPの超長期的影響はどのくらいなのか，まだその確証はないので今後，まだまだ研究を続けていきたい。

7. シンポジウム

谷本：ポストコロナとサステナビリティ，SDGsに関して，多様な角度から議論をしていただいた。サステナビリティ課題については，数十年にわたってグローバルに議論が展開されており，日本でもここ数年SDGsブームが広がっている。今回の新型コロナウイルスの影響を受け，持続可能な発展にかかわる議論は変質しているのか。取り組みが進んだ部分，後退している部分はあるのか。また新たな問題がでてきていないか。とくに環境，人権，貧困にかかわる課題はどうか。パンデミック前後での議論の変化についてコメントをいただきたい。

関：大きく言えば為すべきことは変わらないが，黒田さんが話された包摂的な社会の必要性は今回のコロナにより炙り出された問題点であり，そのプライオリティが強まってきていると思う。しかし，まだ具体的に大きな企業行動の変化に直結してはいない。

　経団連によるアンケート調査でも，企業はやはり「環境」や「エネルギー」への取り組みが多い。目標1「貧困をなくそう」への取り組みは少ないが，実は企業が貢献できる部分は多くあり，そこへの気付きがこれから増えてくるかと思う。

今津：今回のパンデミックが始まった際に，SDGsも含めた動きが止まってしまうのではないかと危惧したが，新聞記事などを追いかけていると反対に動きが加速していると感じ，安心した。

振り返ると，2015年のSDGsやパリ協定の採択で，潮目が変わったと言われている。また，パンデミック直前の2019年には，国連「気候行動サミット」でのグレタ・トゥーンベリさんによるスピーチや，世界中で若者が気候ストライキを行うなど，政治や制度改革への働きかけがあったことで，このコロナ禍でも止まらずに進んできたのではないか。

黒田：自治体でも「SDGs未来都市」などのように前向きに取り組んでいるところも多いが，新型コロナ対応で多忙を極めている自治体では，SDGsどころではないという現状もあると聞いている。

　昨年4，5月の緊急事態宣言時は，誰もが大変な状況であったと思うが，コロナ禍のニューノーマルにおいて，これまで何となくブームのような存在だったSDGsが注目されつつある。SDGsの取り組みが，今後さらに高まってくるのではないか。

谷本：関さんが，2020年10月発表の経団連によるアンケート調査結果を示されたが，実際の調査時期は，昨年4，5月の緊急事態宣言時の頃か。コロナに関する設問もあるのか。

関：調査は2020年6月頃の依頼，8月頃の回収であったと思う。コロナに関しては，緊急事態の中で取り急ぎどのようなことをしているか，という設問が中心で，医療用防護服を作っているなど，とりあえずの危機対応のリアクションが多かった。今日論じているような，大きな変化にはまだ結びつかない設問が多かった。

谷本：サステナビリティ課題をどのように戦略に組み込んでいるかという設問には，各社経営戦略の重要な課題として一生懸命に取り組んでいる，と答えている。しかし，コロナの影響が1年たって，SDGsへの取り組みに変化はあるか。

関：コロナの影響がない企業はないと思うが，だからと言って SDGs どころではない，という話ではない。例えば，日本の企業は今，脱炭素への取り組みを加速している。

　今津さんのお話にあったように，サプライチェーンの中でカーボンゼロが求められる状況になっている。2030 年を意識した対応を求められ，TCFD で戦略情報の開示も迫られる。足元のコロナ禍への対応と，両方を並行的に進めざるを得ない状況にあると思う。

岡本：社会性を収益性・成長性と並んだ企業目標とするということは，社会性を戦略に組み込んでいくという考え方に繋がる。そういう考え方をする企業が増えているように見えるが，実際は，どう戦略に組み込んでいけばいいのかが分からない企業が多いのでは。

　今津さんから紹介された凸版印刷の事例は企業戦略への組み込み方がわかり興味深かった。

福川：ある市場調査によると，パンデミックにより仕事は止まったが給与は支給された世帯で，例えば 40 歳代では給付金支給によって収入が増え，若い世代では衝動買いが増えた，という回答がある。生活に困っていない世代の行動は，SDGs とは逆の方向へいっている。

　貧困層と富裕層のギャップを少なくするにも，インターネットによるサーベイでは回答できない人々，例えばシングルペアレントの家庭における実際の生活状況をもっと知る必要がある。見えている状況が 100％の姿ではないという点を注意しておかなければならない。

谷本：インターネットのサーベイは，そもそもそこにアクセスできない人々の声が聞けない，という問題がある。

福川：システムにはまっていない，いわゆる社会的弱者に関して SDGs のゴールは多くある。その点がきちんと捉えられていないのでは。

谷本：この 1，2 年の中で，サステナビリティ課題の重要性が再認識されたことがわかる動きがある。脱炭素だけではなく，もっと広い視点で企業評価を行う動きがソーシャルファイナンスの分野で広がってきている。ソーシャルインパクトの評価や議論は，日本の中でも少しずつ出てきている。

　また，黒田さんの報告にあったように，課題解決にはさまざまなセクターが連携し合うことも少し前からある議論だが，特に貧困層などなかなか手の届かないところに，NPO/NGO が中心となって連携を強めていく動きが見えてきていると思う。

　ここまでの議論により，サステナビリティ課題の重要性が再認識され，脱炭素だけではなく，環境・社会も含めた ESG 投資の視点が広がってきていること。投資家や消費者といった市場のプレイヤーが変化していること。さらには，社会的弱者や貧困層の課題は，さまざまなセクターとの連携の中で模索している動きがあるということ，といった点が今回のコロナにより明確に見えてきたと思う。

黒田：福島の NPO 法人「しんせい」は，コロナ以前の非常に早い段階からステイクホルダーと連携して活動を進めてきた。2015 年の SDGs 採択以降，障害者の雇用づくりから，再生可能エネルギー導入や食品ロスをなくすための加工工場づくりなど，広がりをもってきている。これは SDGs という共通目標によって繋がりを広げた好事例であるが，ただそういう団体がまだ多いわけではない。

質問ー島本晴一郎（京都 CSR 研究会）：一般に，商品選考の際にはまず価格，次にデザイン・機能・耐久性，最終的には意味価値，いわゆるシンボルとしての意味が働いてくると言われている。消費者行動にはどのような影響が出ているのか。

福川：コロナ以前からエシカル消費があるが，

消費者が児童労働のないフェアトレード製品や有機野菜などといったエシカル商品を選ばない理由として，まず一番に価格があげられる。しかしその一方で，消費者個人にとって意味のある消費においては，価格は判断基準から外される。一辺倒に価格が関係している，ということではない。意味を見出す消費者にとっては，価格に関しての感情は鈍化されるという傾向にある。

　コロナ禍での消費の変化については，J-marketing という市場会社によると，40歳以上の富裕層の消費パターンで，贅沢品の購入が増えたとある。コロナ禍で外出機会が減り，宅内時間が増えたためと考えられるが，この状況も世帯の所得によって大きく異なる。

島本：中小企業にも SDGs はかなり浸透しており，大企業は完全に SDGs にシフトしていると感じる。従来，企業戦略の中に CSR ミッションを組み込むのは難しいとされてきたが，このコロナ禍で，SDGs を埋め込み，戦略化していこうという動きが一挙に増えた。また，PDCA を日常的にどう行うか，マネジメントに各社の差が出ている。

　コロナ禍で，ステイクホルダーの中でも従業員と消費者の重要度がかなり上がってきたことは間違いない。労働環境は即，逃れられない問題となり，環境衛生の分野も大きくクローズアップされている。また，共助の意識として，例えば NPO との協働が意識されている。コロナ対応の観点から，SDGs の選択がされているのではないか。

谷本：2021年1月開催の国際シンポジウムの際に，ゴミや環境，貧困などの問題について，今回のコロナを契機に，政府が規制をしっかりすべきという声もあった。

　これまでの SDGs の課題は，基本的に各企業が自発的に取り組み，さまざまな事例が出てきているが，政府の規制についてはどう思われるか。

関：規制よりも，2030年，2050年に向けて何をどうするのかという方向性を，政府が明確に出し，企業や消費者がそれに向かっていくことの方がより重要だと思う。縛るよりむしろ変化を促すような一貫性のある政策メッセージには非常に大きな影響力があり，特にこのトランスフォーメーションの時代には必要不可欠だと思う。

今津：われわれ現場ではサーキュラーエコノミーに向けての動きはスタートしているが，現時点で規制が強すぎて，仕組みを作ろうにも企業だけではできない状況にある。変革のために規制を緩めていくことも含め，政府・省庁と企業のニーズをうまく合わせていけると，本当に進んでいくなと感じる。

黒田：規制をかけた方がいいと思われるものもある。レジ袋の有料化は，規制によって勢いよく進んだ。ただ，どのような政策のもとどのような規制があるといいのか，あるいは規制を緩めた方がいいのか，丁寧に議論をしていく必要があると思う。

　政府がやらなければならないことを企業にだけ押し付けるのではなく，官民がしっかりと連携を取ると同時に他のステイクホルダーが参加できるようなしくみが広がると良いと思う。

岡本：規制として，企業の行動を制限してしまうのはよろしくないと思うが，外からの影響として広義的に捉えると，SDGs はとても良いプラスの影響になっていると思う。

　コロナによって多くの企業が大変な経済的損失を被っているわけだが，うまく対処できた企業とできない企業との差が広がっている。

　実はコロナがなくても，駄目だった企業は駄目だったのではないか。

福川：ここで期待したいのは，若い世代の起業

家や NPO といった，イノベーションを引っ張っていく小さな組織や集団を，もっとバックアップできるような世間になっていくこと。

例えば，食品にアクセスできない貧困層の問題が，コロナによって世界中で多く出てきた。アメリカでは，食品ロスと余っている食品の在庫を組み合わせて貧困層へ配るというネットワークを，大学生の起業家が作ったケースがある。そのような取り組みをサポートする ESG 投資が日本でも多く出てくるといいなと思う。

谷本：ソーシャルアントレプレナーの新しい動きもみられる。また既存の組織においてもアントレプレナーシップをもって，新しいビジネスを始めることができる。それは政府の中でも同じだと思うが，そのような発想も必要になってくると思う。

質問－吉田賢一（早稲田大学ビジネス・ファイナンス研究センター）：今日のお話の中で，ESGへの市場の評価の高まりについてご指摘があったが，直近での自身の検証によると，株式を相互持ち合いしているとか，いわゆる旧来からの外的な声が届きにくい企業ほど ESG や CSR 活動をしていない，という傾向が出ている。谷本先生の分析でもかなり以前より指摘されているが，硬直的な企業というのは今後も一部残っていくのでは。そのような企業には，外的な働きかけは非常に難しいのではないかと個人的に思っている。

今回のコロナを契機に変わっていく余地があるのか，それともさらに二極化が続いていくのか。

関：アンケートをとってみると，企業が今，最も強く意識しているステイクホルダーは投資家である。外国人株主の比率の高まりによって，たとえ国内の株主がおとなしくても，投資家の声は，企業行動の変化を促す。

日本でもようやく「2050 年カーボンニュートラル宣言」が出たし，何もせずに手をこまねいている企業は少ないとは思うが，それでも吉田さんのおっしゃるように，経団連会員企業の中でも，環境や人権への取り組みにおいて，動かない企業とどんどん対応を進化させる企業との差は拡大し，二極化が進んでいると感じる。

谷本：本日の議論はここまでにしたいと思う。ご参加いただいた方々，スピーカーの方々，本日はどうもありがとうございました。

(1)　「第 2 回企業行動憲章に関するアンケート調査結果─ウィズ・コロナにおける企業行動憲章の実践状況─」2020 年 10 月 13 日　（一社）日本経済団体連合会。

(2)　NPO 法人「人間の安全保障フォーラム」編，高須幸雄編著（2019）『SDGs と日本：誰も取り残されないための「人間の安全保障指標」』明石書店。

(3)　https://www3.nhk.or.jp/news/special/coronavirus/difficulty/detail/detail_01.html

(4)　https://prtimes.jp/main/html/rd/p/000000051.000019571.html（最終訪問日　2021.4.5）

(5)　https://www3.nhk.or.jp/news/html/20201114/k10012711801000.html（最終訪問日　2021.4.5）

(6)　2020 年 8 月 27 日「みんなの SDGs」COVID-19 と SDGs シリーズ　第 2 回オンラインセミナー「SDGs と新型コロナ：在日外国人を取り残さないために（生活編）」

(7)　https://prtimes.jp/main/html/searchrlp/company_id/18247（最終訪問日　2021.4.5）

(8)　https://migrants.jp/user/news/479/zx-77azhkv_1ebwqkn9xot4st813u0_1.pdf（最終訪問日　2021.4.5）

(9)　Sheth, J. (2020) 'Impact of Covid-19 on consumer behavior: Will the old habits return or die?,' *Journal of Business Research*, 117: 280-283.

(10)　TDB-CAREE：消費者心理調査　https://www7.econ.hit-u.ac.jp/tdb-caree/survey/

(11)　総務省，家計調査　https://www.stat.go.jp/data/kakei/index.html（JMR 生活総合研究所　https://www.jmrlsi.co.jp/membership/premium/concept/report/economy/sokuho210316.html より）

(12)　PWC「世界の消費者意識調査 2020」https://www.pwc.com/jp/ja/knowledge/thoughtleadership/2020/assets/pdf/consumer-insights-survey.pdf

Building Public Relations through an Art Place
——A Case Study of Benesse Art Site Naoshima

Makiko Kawakita
Professor, Faculty of Business Administration, Nanzan University

Yasushi Sonobe
Professor, Faculty of Sociology, Toyo University

Key words : art management, art place, stakeholders, media, public relations, corporate social responsibility, philanthropy

[Abstract]

This study examines why companies become involved with art as a media, using the case of Benesse Art Site Naoshima (BASN). BASN is an art place that is visited by many art fans worldwide and was started by a single company. Previous studies have shown that the focus of stakeholder theory has shifted from managing to building relationships. Arts management research has indicated that corporate involvement with the arts has a positive impact on internal assets as well as external stakeholders; however, the details remain unclear. Thus, this study aims to reveal the function that an art place—a place that internalises art—plays as media to build relationships between a company and its stakeholders through a case study of BASN.

In-depth interviews were conducted with people associated with BASN; the data was used to examine the impact that BASN had on its relationships with diverse stakeholders. The role of the art place as media was evaluated and three functions were identified: the function of expanding its reach to stakeholders whom it did not usually come into contact with; the function of facilitating deeper messages to each stakeholder, which enabled employees to have a perspective on the future; and of building network-based, rather than dyadic, relationships. A community was born from the long-term creation of a networked relationship with art as a hub. Although it required substantial time and effort, art succeeded as a powerful communication tool.

Reviewed Article (Received January 27th 2021 / Accepted May 16th 2021)

1. Introduction

For a company to be a going concern, it must build and maintain good relationships with its various stakeholders. Therefore, companies often use communication to build relationships with their stakeholders. In recent years, attention has focused on the benefits of art in business, and one of these benefits is building public relations through art places.

This study reveals the function of an art place, in other words a place that internalises art, as media to build relationships between a company and its stakeholders through the case of Benesse Art Site Naoshima (BASN).

BASN is an art project funded mainly by Benesse Holdings, which has attracted worldwide media attention and brought tourists from all over the world to Naoshima.

2. BASN

BASN is the collective name for the art activities conducted on three remote islands in Japan, namely, Naoshima, Teshima and Inujima. The project aims to incorporate modern art into the unique landscape of these islands. The project is run by Benesse Holdings, Inc., and the Fukutake Foundation, which was established through donations by the family of the company's founder, Tetsuhiko Fukutake. Benesse Group is a Japanese company with annual sales of 448.6 billion yen (March 2020), which focuses on correspondence education for children.

In 1986, Soichiro Fukutake took over the company, and since 1992, he has been spearheading this project. Thirty years have been spent carefully constructing the art facility on Naoshima to create site-specific modern art museums and groups of works. 'Site-specific' refers to the artwork that expresses the characteristics of a specific location (Oki, n.d.). Presently, there are 22 facilities spanning five islands, along with many outdoor displays (BASN, n.d.).

The basic policy is 'to create one art space in the middle of the landscape of the Seto Inland Sea Region over time, and thus, by combining modern art and architecture in the nature and unique culture of each island, to create novel spaces'. Such places provoke visitors to think about the corporate philosophy of the Benesse Group, 'Benesse—Well-Being'. BASN affirms the building and maintenance of long-lasting relationships as follows: 'In all our on-going activities, we are committed to fostering a relationship of mutual growth between art and the region, aiming to make a positive contribution to the local communities' (BASN, n.d.).

In 2000, Naoshima was selected as one of Conde Nast Traveller's Seven Wonders, and in 2010, the Setouchi Triennale, or Art Setouchi (collectively referred to below as 'Art Setouchi'), began in the area centred around Naoshima. In 2019, Art Setouchi became the prime destination for National Geographic Traveller (U.K.). Today, art lovers from around the world visit Naoshima to appreciate the modern art.

3. | Literature review and research question

Several fields have studied the involvement of the business sector with art. Advertising research has studied sponsorship as a type of advertising activity. Sponsorship refers to investments into causes or events that are carried out to support the goals of any firm or marketing agency (Gardner & Shuman, 1988). However, sponsorship research is far less prevalent in art than in sports (Sonobe & Kawakita, 2020), and the effects of art-specific sponsorship remain unclear.

Few studies have examined art in the field of public relations; however, in the case of BASN, because Benesse has built long-term relationships with its stakeholders—such as local residents, artists and employees—through the art places, it can be studied within the context of stakeholder theory in public relations and informed by art management research as well as art and media studies.

3-1. Stakeholder theory

Stakeholder research began when Freeman and Reed (1983) argued for a paradigm shift where, instead of companies focusing on stockholders only, attention should be paid to all the stakeholders. Subsequently, studies classifying and identifying stakeholders (e.g. Frederick, Davis, & Post, 1988) and studies on the different qualities of their relationships (e.g. Payne, Ballantyne, & Christopher, 2005) began to develop. Further, discussions emerged for the shift from managing to building relationships (Halal, 2001).

Relatedly, Lozano (2005) proposed the term 'relational corporation'. This term refers to companies that do not manage their relationship with stakeholders but instead change their approach towards building a relationship together. This approach includes network-based and process-oriented methods. Network-based methods suggest that instead of the past firm-centred dyadic relationship of 'influence—be influenced', complex modern society is perceived as a structure of networks, and companies take on the perspective of co-responsibility, for society with the stakeholders.

Process-oriented methods refer to building trust and commitment through exchange and conversation with partners. 'It is within this process that we confront the inevitable differences and conflicts that in practice always affect stakeholder relationships. Building such complex relationships means narrating, explaining, drafting, understanding and giving them meaning, considering the interests, values and principles that are at stake' (Lozano, 2005, p. 70).

Conventionally, the values that stakeholders pursue are not the same as those of companies; thus, a conflict is assumed. Here, Schormair and Gilbert (2021) summarised how value conflicts with stakeholders are perceived. They classified values based on whether value is perceived as monism or pluralism. The former case includes the following three stances: financial value, shared value (Porter & Kramer, 2006; 2011) and aggregate happiness (Jones and Felps, 2013a; 2013b). The latter case assumes that each stakeholder is oriented towards different values. From this perspective, the challenge is that a concrete path towards relationship building is not clearly presented.

Presently, research on consensus-building process in political science and stakeholder theory in business administration are merging. Schormair and Gilbert (2021) saw the consensus-building processes as agonistic and deliberative approaches and presented a five-step framework for a comprehensive approach that is neither of these. They also indicated that in the field of stakeholder management, few studies deal with the aspects of shared communication.

Cutlip, Center and Broom (2006: 5) stated that '[p]ublic relations is the management function that establishes and maintains mutually beneficial relationships between an organisation and the public on whom its success or failure depends'. BASN is a place where diverse stakeholders hold long-lasting dialogues about the complex problems of modern society through art. In other words, it is a place to practice building public relations; Benesse thus embodies Lozano's (2005) 'relational corporation' through an art place.

To practice building public relations, relationships with each stakeholder must be built through direct communication, and indirect communication with each stakeholder must be actualised with mass media as the mode. For the latter, mass media such as newspapers and magazines are also important stakeholders.

3-2. Art management research

Compared to other countries, Japan's national budget for culture is as low as 104 billion yen, which is approximately a fifth of the budget of France, the country with the highest budget for culture in the world. Moreover, private donations from the private sector are minimal owing to the lack of tax benefits (CDI, 2018). Kawashima (2012) observed that problems in Japanese cultural administration include a lack of policy and management professionals. In such a situation, companies have been supporting the arts as a form of philanthropy and have played a role in cultural promotion in Japan. To explain the reasons for this investment in arts support by companies, we should consider the benefits to the company as well as the cause of social contribution.

In the field of art management, sponsorship and partnership have been studied in the context of acquiring support for art organisations. Event partnerships between companies and art organisations not only improve external brand recognition but also have an impact on the internal corporate assets.

Comunian (2009) attempted to explain the implications of business investment trends in art from a business perspective and presented a new conceptual framework for why corporations are becoming more involved in art and culture. There is a competitive advantage at three levels. The first is the competitive advantage that is brought about by the effects of sponsorship on customers and other external stakeholders, such as image transfer and improvement. Furthermore, arts sponsorship is the best method to attract influential people that other sponsorships cannot. The second level is defined by the possibility for the company to generate competitive advantage in its product market. The third level is the effect on the internal assets of the company. It has a positive impact on human resources, not only on visible assets such as artworks but also on the interaction with artists. This effect on assets provides a future competitive advantage.

Lewandowska (2015) demonstrated that partnership collaboration with the arts, rather than mere sponsorship by companies, increases creativity and learning and enhances positive relationships with communities and stakeholders.

These studies reveal that internal corporate assets are positively affected when companies not only provide financial support alone but also build interactive relationships with art events and organisations. However, there has been a lack of clarity regarding the exact nature of this positive impact.

3-3. Art and media

Generally, we perceive the term 'media' as a means to mediate communication between entities. The broad definition of (information) media refers to all tools and devices that not only transmit but also accumulate and process information (Mikami, 2004). A more detailed definition includes being a carrier that transmits information and a function that represents it.

Depending on the type of carrier, media can be divided into four types: spatial media (plazas, theatres, stadiums, indoor/outdoor event spaces, etc.), portable media (newspapers, magazines, CDs, etc.), wired media (landline tele-

phones, optical fibre networks, etc.) and wireless (radio wave) media (television broadcasts, wireless LAN, etc.) (Mikami, 2004). Based on this classification, an art place is categorised as spatial media internalising information content constituted by modern art. An artwork alone would be insufficient, but its incorporation into a site enables it to function as media.

Fukutake (2016) discussed the function of art as media and noted that in the process of community revitalisation through art practiced at BASN, art and architecture function as 'media' that build a relationship between urban youths and rural elders. He also argued that 'in literature, music and film, the creator is the subject, enforcing their opinions on the recipient; however, modern art may be the only media that lets the recipient be the subject' (36). According to Fukutake, this island with its scattering of modern art is a medium that allows recipients to be the active subject. The aspect that differentiates BASN from a typical art museum is how the whole island acts as a spatial medium through the scattering of artwork.

3-4. Research question

In public relations, the goal is to maintain a healthy relationship with stakeholders. Additionally, although arts management research identifies the positive impact of collaboration with the arts on the external and internal stakeholders of a company, the specific effects thereof are unclear. BASN's role as media is to build relationships with diverse stakeholders. Thus, the following research question arises: What impact has the art place, with its corporate support, had on each stakeholder?

4. Methodology

We conducted in-depth interviews with those in positions deeply involved with BASN at that time to examine what impact BASN had on the relationships with diverse stakeholders.

The interviewees were Soichiro Fukutake (Honorary Adviser of Benesse Holdings Inc., BASN Founder and Chairman of Fukutake Foundation), Kenjiro Kaneshiro (Director of Fukutake Foundation), Ryoji Kasahara (President and CEO of Naoshima Cultural Village Co., Ltd.), Shigenori Fujii (Secretary of Town-Naoshima Tourism Association) and Kaori Sakamoto (then Manager of Benesse Holdings, Public Relations/Investor Relations Department). The interviews were held over three days between 31 January and 13 April 2019. The main questions were 'How have you been involved with various stakeholders through BASN?' and 'What effects has BASN had?'.

5. Findings from the interviews

This art place was created through the passion of Soichiro Fukutake, the Honorary Adviser of Benesse. His drive was the resistance to negative aspects of excessive modernisation and urbanisation. Modern society has sacrificed rural areas and nature for urban lifestyles. Although Naoshima permitted a copper smelter to be built 100 years ago, pollution from the sulphurous acid gas released from the smelter had stripped the mountains of

their vegetation. In Teshima, located next to Naoshima, a large amount of illegally discarded toxic materials were discovered. Inujima has also been polluted with soot released from the copper smelter. To raise the question of 'Is this society acceptable?' with respect to this negative history, Fukutake borrowed the power of art. According to Fukutake, artistic activities lead to 'good community-building'.

The company's name Benesse means 'well-being'. Naoshima is a place where their corporate philosophy, 'What does it mean to live well?', can be contemplated. As Picasso painted Guernica, Fukutake is questioning the social issues by considering 'well-being' as part of an art project.

6. Effects on various stakeholders

Based on the interviews, we examined the impact BASN had on the relationships with various stakeholders.

The project nurtured and sustained positive opinions about the company in employees, thus leading them to stay with the job longer. Additionally, employees' perspectives were widened and the organisational culture of the company became more creative. As per the interviews, employees knew that Benesse is a company driven by its corporate philosophy of 'well-being' (Kaneshiro and Sakamoto). New employees and managers experienced the culture at BASN during their training, and this instilled in them the idea that BASN is a place to think about 'well-being'. Employees also appreciated the company more when they heard about Naoshima from others outside the company (Kasahara). Naoshima exists as emotional support, which has kept some employees from leaving the company (Sakamoto). 'Each business is a part of many social activities, right? ⋯ So, a company can't last unless it has the ability to see society from the business perspective and business from the social perspective' (Kaneshiro). In its relationship with society, a company develops an eye for its own business. Further, Fukutake believes that cultural activity is one way for companies to improve their creativity. However, the present day-to-day contact with art is very infrequent.

With respect to the job market, clients and business partners, the effects included not only gaining recognition but also understanding the corporate philosophy, screening for shared values and acquiring trust as a company with social responsibility. It was argued that by letting aspiring employees experience Art Site Naoshima, the company could observe if they could understand the corporate philosophy and be a good fit within the company (Sakamoto and Kasahara). As for clients, 'Chinese managers often hear about Naoshima and wish to collaborate' (Fukutake). With important clients and business partners, having them see BASN enables them to understand Benesse's corporate philosophy and gain trust (Sakamoto and Kasahara).

With respect to investors, particularly those from overseas, it improved recognition and corporate image. At domestic ordinary general shareholders' meetings, it leads to favourable support (Fukutake). Even foreign investors who do not know about the company's

educational products, such as Shinken Zemi correspondence education program, are familiar with Benesse as the owner of BASN. Additionally, the existence of Naoshima may 'improve the image' of the company (Sakamoto).

There are 700–800 media interviews yearly (Kaneshiro). As mentioned earlier, world-renowned newspapers and magazines visit the island for interviews. This aspect improves the trust of business partners and investors. However, for customers, products and BASN are not well-connected. Not many customers seem to know that Shinken Zemi and BASN are both run by Benesse. In that sense, BASN is not familiar to customers (Kasahara and Sakamoto).

For the community, the use of the whole island rather than simply a museum as an art place increases the number of people who are involved with artists, people on the island and tourists. Local elderly people are being revitalised and regaining the energy and pride that they once lost due to population decline, pollution and industrial wastes. 'More than any other media, modern art awakens people and changes the community. No one else in the world has noticed this. I mean, it brought life to old people in this remote little village' (Fukutake).

'When artists decide to create something that only exists here, they dig up the long history and livelihood of the island and people. When artists research this history, it reminds the people of the island of their own history' (Kasahara). 'The biggest damage from the industrial problems that have been going on for half a century on Teshima Island is that residents have lost their pride. This is the reason why Fukutake decided to build an art museum over there (Teshima Art Museum). We aimed to change the community with culture and art. With Teshima Art Museum being built and becoming the main venue for Art Setouchi, people remember the beauty of their own island and regain their pride' (Kaneshiro).

'Without being asked, many island residents go out of their way to talk to tourists, share their knowledge of the artworks and experience interacting with artists and tell stories about how art has changed the community. Some may provide tips on how to take photos of the artwork (those for which photography is permitted). People of the island will drive lost tourists to the destinations by car instead of just giving them the map directions' (Fujii).

7. | Results and conclusions

Based on the data gained from this study, we determined the functions of company-supported art places as media (see Figure 1). Benesse has succeeded in community-building—thinking about society together through BASN—and in building relationships with stakeholders. Hence, the following three functions are evident.

The first is the function of expanding its reach to stakeholders whom they usually do not come in contact with. If BASN had created a regular art museum instead of an art site, they would not have been able to make contact with the local people with whom they interacted to make artwork. As the appeal of BASN attracts foreign media companies, its

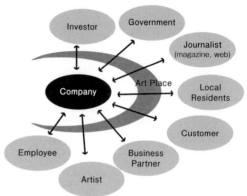

Figure 1 Art Place as Media

Source: Created by the authors based on Freeman (1984) and Sonobe (2014)

international recognition has notably increased. By incorporating the modern art preferred by those with high incomes who could become investors and the management class who could become business partners, important stakeholders can be approached.

The second function is facilitating deeper messages to each stakeholder. Simply trying to express the corporate philosophy of 'well-being', to others in words alone is nothing more than a one-sided message that is unlikely to arouse emotion. However, in a place that incorporates modern art allowing recipients to be the subject, people's ears and eyes can be opened, and they can develop feelings for various social issues. Instead of trying to tell, it waits for others' feelings to be evoked. This is a time-consuming process, but they continue with consistent patience. Even if this message includes a strong argument for resistance, it can provide room to think together through the unique refinement of art.

This function also allows employees to find meaning in their existence in society. They are exposed to social issues through a place to think about 'well-being', thus allowing them to nurture perspectives for the future. This aspect also leads them to think about their own company. Why does art enable this? Art not only has the power to 'affect people emotionally' but also the property of 'critically analysing existing values and discovering new perspectives'.

The third function is to build relationships based on networks. In traditional public relations, activities are aimed towards specific stakeholders with, for example, the relationship of 'influencing-influenced' in the corporate-centred perspective. However, with BASN, the framework enables interaction throughout the whole island; thus, various stakeholders, such as artists, local people, young visitors and international fans of the artwork, become connected, thus formulating a communication channel. This aspect builds a network-based relationship where trust and commitment are born.

8. Practical and social implications

With respect to art support by a company, relationships leading to trust can be built with new stakeholders not only by providing funds but also by building an art place that values the communication process. In this study, the case of BASN shows that an art place can play a role as a medium. It takes immense commitment for a company to continue expressing a consistent message over a long period through their activities. Therefore, generalising this approach for other companies may be difficult.

Nonetheless, this community revitalisation model is called the 'Naoshima method', thereby referring to the process below and has garnered interest overseas in China and elsewhere.

> Artists create work that can only exist on this land with a message critical of modernity. Island residents become involved. Artwork remains when artists leave, and young people visit the island to see the artwork. Seniors begin to tell their stories about the artists, surprising young people. This situation is very interesting. Soon seniors of the island will begin to talk about the history and culture of the island as well (Fukutake, 2016: 45).

If business owners can continue to invest their will and funds in this activity and hold dialogues with artists on an equal ground, this method may be implemented by other companies. However, one should be ready for such a long-term involvement. The social implication is that one company's work through art can change regional communities. To this end, it must be process-oriented, as in this case. This study focused on interviews with those at Benesse, but we hope to continue this work by interviewing external artists, municipalities and media companies.

Acknowledgements

We would like to thank those who generously participated in the interviews for this study. We were funded by Grant-in-Aid for Scientific Research (C) 20K01946 and Nanzan University Pache Research Subsidy I-A-2 for the 2020 academic year. We thus extend our most sincere appreciation to them.

〈References〉

Benesse Art Site Naoshima [BASN] (n.d.) Retrieved from https://benesse-artsite.jp/.

CDI (2018) Report on comparative research on cultural policies in other countries, Available at https://www.bunka.go.jp/tokei_hakusho_shuppan/tokeichosa/pdf/r1393024_04.pdf, Accessed 2021.5.24 (in Japanese).

Comunian, R. (2009) 'Toward a New Conceptual Framework for Business Investments in the Arts: Some Examples from Italy,' *Journal of Arts Management, Law, and Society*, Vol. 39, No. 3, pp. 200-220

Cutlip, S. M., Center, A. H. and Broom, G. M. (2006) *Effective Public Relations* (9th ed), Pearson (international ed).

Frederick, W. C., Davis, K. and Post, J. E. (1988) *Business and society: Corporate strategy, public policy, ethics*, New York: McGraw-Hill Companies.

Freeman, R. E. and Reed, D. L. (1983) 'Stockholders and stakeholders: A new perspective on corporate governance,' *California Management Review*, Vol. 25, No. 3, pp. 88-106.

—— (1984) *Strategic Management: A Stakeholder Approach*, Pitman Publishing.

Fukutake, S. (2016) From Benesse art site Naoshima to Art Setouchi. in S. Fukutake & F. Kitagawa, *From Naoshima to Art Setouchi: Art has changed the region*, Gendai Kikakushitsu (in Japanese).

Gardner, M. P. and Shuman, P. (1988) 'Sponsorships and small businesses,' *Journal of Small Business Management*, Vol. 26, No. 4, pp. 44-52.

Halal, W. E. (2001) 'The collaborative enterprise: A stakeholder model uniting profitability and responsibility,' *Journal of Corporate Citizenship*, No. 2, pp. 27-42.

Jones, T. M. and Felps, W. (2013a) 'Shareholder wealth maximization and social welfare: A utilitarian critique,' *Business Ethics Quarterly*, Vol. 23, No. 2, pp. 207-238.

—— and Felps, W. (2013b) 'Stakeholder happiness enhancement: A neo-utilitarian objective for the modern corporation,' *Business Ethics Quarterly*, Vol. 23, No. 3, pp. 349-379.

Kawashima, N. (2012) 'Corporate support for the arts in Japan: Beyond emulation of the Western models,' *International Journal of Cultural Policy*, Vol. 18, No. 3, pp. 295-307.

Lewandowska, K. (2015) 'From sponsorship to partnership in arts and business relations,' *Journal of Arts Management, Law, and Society*, Vol. 45, No. 1, pp. 33-50.

Lozano, J. M. (2005) 'Towards the relational corporation: From managing stakeholder relationships to building stakeholder relationships (waiting for Copernicus),' *Corporate Governance*, Vol. 5, No. 2, pp. 60-77.

Mikami, S. (2004) *Invitation to media communication studies*, Gakubunsha (in Japanese).

Oki, K. (n.d.) Art notebook. Available at https://bijutsutecho.com/artwiki/95, Accessed 2021.5.24 (in Japanese).

Payne, A., Ballantyne, D. and Christopher, M. (2005) 'A stakeholder approach to relationship marketing strategy: The development and use of the "six markets" model,' *European Journal of Marketing*, Vol. 39, No. 7/8, pp. 855-871.

Porter, M. E. and Kramer, M. R. (2006) 'Strategy and Society: The link between competitive advantage and corporate social responsibility,' *Harvard Business Review*, Vol. 84, No. 12, pp. 78-92.

—— and Kramer, M. R. (2011) 'Creating Shared Value,' *Harvard Business Review*, Vol. 89, No. 1/2, pp. 62-77.

Schormair, M. J. L. and Gilbert, D. U. (2021) 'Creating value by sharing values: Managing stakeholder value conflict in the face of pluralism through discursive justification,' *Business Ethics Quarterly*, Vol. 31, No. 1, pp. 1-36.

Sonobe, Y. (2014) Stakeholder and Corporate Social Responsibility, in Ibuki, Y., Kawakita, M., Kitami, K., Sekiya, N. and Sonobe, Y. (eds.) *Introduction to Public Relations: Theory and Practice*, pp. 25-37, Yuhikaku (in Japanese).

—— and Kawakita, M. (2020) 'The Prestige Effects of Sponsorship on Attitudes toward Corporate Brands and Art Events,' *Japan Forum of Business and Society Annals*, No. 9, pp. 42-58.

Japan Forum of Business and Society Annals, No.10, pp. 41-55, 2021   41

Chinese CSR Report Rating
——Symbolic or Substantial?

Xinwu He

PhD Candidate in Accounting, Durham University Business School

Key words : Chinese CSR Report Rating, CSR reporting, CSR assurance, China, Case study

【Abstract】

This case study examines the nature of the Chinese Corporate Social Responsibility (CSR) Report Rating, a local CSR-related practice recently developed and provided by a government-affiliated research institution. The past decade has witnessed the rapid growth of CSR reporting in China and the development of the CSR Report Rating. However, the extant literature remains inconclusive regarding (1) whether the Rating can effectively enhance the credibility of CSR reports and (2) why Chinese companies, particularly State-owned Enterprises (SOEs), prefer the Rating. This paper fills the research gaps through an engagement-based case study. Evidence collected for the case study includes interview data and documents. A key finding is the symbolic nature of the Chinese CSR Report Rating. It is more like an extension or a "variant" of CSR consulting, a mechanism for companies' CSR strategy, and a business image enhancement tool, rather than an alternative to CSR assurance.

1. Introduction

The past decade has witnessed an increasing demand for corporate non-financial disclosures from investors, shareholders, customers, and other stakeholders (Shabana, Buchholtz, and Carroll, 2017). The increasing demand has led to the proliferation of corporate social responsibility (CSR)/sustainability reporting covering an organisation's economic, environmental, and social impacts and positive or negative contributions to sustainable development (GRI, 2016). The number of Chinese companies reporting on CSR has increased dramatically during the past decade. According to Yin et al. (2019), 739 Chinese companies reported CSR in 2009, and the number increased to 2,089 in 2019. This increase has been primarily driven by governmental CSR reporting guidelines since 2008. For example, the State-owned Assets Supervision and Administration Commission of the State Council (SASAC)[1] published Recommendations for Central Enterprises[2] on Fulfilling Social Responsibility (SASAC, 2008). The Recommendations encouraged Central Enterprises to establish CSR reporting systems. In 2009, the SASAC required all

Reviewed Article (Received February 13th 2021 / Accepted May 16th 2021)

Central Enterprises to publish CSR reports within three years (Zhu, Liu, and Lai, 2016).

With the proliferation of CSR reporting in China, a local CSR-related practice has been developed: the Chinese CSR Report Rating provided by the Chinese Expert Committee on CSR Report Rating. This practice is broadly regarded as a mechanism to enhance the credibility of CSR reporting. Many Chinese CSR reporting companies, particularly state-owned enterprises (SOEs), adopt the Rating annually. However, it remains unclear (1) whether the Rating can effectively enhance the credibility of CSR reporting and (2) why the Chinese companies prefer the Rating. There is a lack of research exploring the nature, process, and effectiveness of the Chinese CSR Report Rating within the extant literature.

This research examines the nature of the Chinese CSR Report Rating and its effectiveness in enhancing the credibility of CSR reporting. An engagement-based qualitative case study approach was adopted. The evidence collected for the case study included interview data (primary data) and documentary data (secondary data). A thematic analysis of the evidence was conducted. The findings reveal that the CSR Report Rating is more like an extension or a "variant" of CSR consulting service, a mechanism for companies' CSR strategy, and a corporate image tool, rather than an alternative to CSR assurance[3]. Therefore, its effectiveness in enhancing the credibility of CSR reporting is questionable.

This case study makes several contributions. First, it represents an early attempt to investigate the Chinese CSR Report Rating practice overlooked by the extant literature. It provides evidence through a fieldwork-based qualitative study, responding to the call for more engagement research within CSR/ sustainability accounting and accountability area (Adams and Larrinaga, 2019). Second, this study contributes to a comprehensive and nuanced understanding of the Chinese CSR Report Rating. It clears up the ambiguity about the purpose and nature of the Rating by suggesting that it is more like an extension or a "variant" of CSR consulting service rather than an alternative to CSR assurance. Third, this study has important practical implications. The symbolic nature of the Rating implies that the credibility of Chinese CSR reports is doubtful. There is an urgent demand for credibility-enhancing mechanisms (for example, mandatory CSR assurance) for Chinese CSR reporting.

The Reminder of the paper is organised as follows. Chapter 2 provides a literature review on the development of CSR reporting in China and the origin, purpose, and process of the Chinese CSR Report Rating. Chapter 3 describes the research methods. Chapter 4 discusses the findings from the case study analysis and highlights the Rating's symbolic nature. The last chapter concludes this case study with research contributions, limitations, and avenues for further research.

2. | Literature Review

CSR reporting has recently become nearly universally adopted and is considered the global norm (KPMG, 2020). China has achieved a CSR reporting rate of 78% in 2020, slightly higher than the global average (77%) (KPMG, 2020). This higher-than-average rate marks a significant growth of CSR reporting in China over the past decade, compared to the CSR reporting rate (nearly 60%) in 2011 (KPMG, 2011). The development of CSR reporting in China features considerable governmental influence, which is reflected in three aspects (Li and Belal, 2018; Shen, Wu, and Chand, 2017; Zhao, 2012; Zhu, Liu, and Lai, 2016; Zhu and Zhang, 2015): (1) the Chinese government's leading role in driving CSR reporting; (2) SOEs' pioneering role in implementing CSR reporting; and (3) the domination of experts with governmental or quasi-governmental backgrounds in the CSR consulting and assurance market.

With the rapid growth of CSR reporting, there is an increasing concern about the credibility of CSR disclosures, as companies may use CSR reporting as a marketing/greenwashing/image tool (Laufer, 2003; Mahoney et al., 2013; Uyar, Karaman, and Kilic, 2020). Previous literature indicates mechanisms that can enhance the credibility of CSR reporting, including CSR assurance, robust internal control and reporting systems, stakeholder engagement, and internal audit (Simnett, Zhou, and Hoang, 2016). Particularly, CSR assurance is an essential credibility-enhancing mechanism where independent assurance providers are involved and verifying CSR reports. It helps reduce information asymmetry and increase stakeholder confidence in the reliability of CSR disclosures (Boiral and Heras-Saizarbitoria, 2020). The number of companies investing in

CSR assurance worldwide has increased steadily since 2005 (KPMG, 2020). Notably, few Chinese companies currently invest in CSR assurance (KPMG, 2020). According to Yin et al. (2019), only 5.19% of the Chinese CSR reports published in 2019 were assured. This low percentage reveals that most Chinese CSR reporting companies are reluctant to invest in CSR assurance. It further implies that the credibility of Chinese CSR reports is questionable.

The Chinese context has recently witnessed the development of a CSR-related practice perceived as another credibility-enhancing mechanism: the Chinese CSR Report Rating. It is a service provided by the Chinese Expert Committee on CSR Report Rating founded by the Corporate Social Responsibility Research Centre, Chinese Academy of Social Sciences[4] (CASS-CSRRC).

Founded in 2008, CASS-CSRRC is a government-affiliated research institution focusing on CSR in China. It runs research projects on CSR-related topics and publishes research work. Also, CASS-CSRRC is a standards organisation. It has developed The Chinese Corporate Social Responsibility Reporting Guide (CASS-CSR 4.0) (Zhong et al., 2018). Moreover, CASS-CSRRC runs a CSR-related business, providing CSR consulting, report writing, and report rating services. Therefore, CASS-CSRRC plays multiple roles in the CSR area.

In the CSR Report Rating service, CASS-CSRRC works with the Chinese Expert Committee on CSR Report Rating, evaluates the quality of a company's CSR report, and issues a Rating Report with comments and sugges-

Figure 1　The structure of the Chinese Expert Committee on CSR Report Rating

Source: translated and adapted from Chinese Expert Committee on CSR Report Rating (2020, p.6).

tions. The Committee consists of experts from the government, universities, research institutions, and industry associations. For each rating project, the Committee sets up a rating panel. Figure 1 shows the structure of the Committee.

The CSR Report Rating evaluates the quality and management of CSR reporting, aiming at (1) providing CSR reporting entities with professional advice to improve the quality of CSR disclosures and support the implementation of CSR activities; (2) enhancing CSR management through better CSR reporting which facilitates stakeholder dialogue and CSR performance improvement; and (3) facilitating the development of CSR in China (Chinese Expert Committee on CSR Report Rating, 2020). Therefore, the Rating provides reporting companies with professional advice regarding CSR reporting and management. It is essentially an extension or a "variant" of CSR consulting service.

Previous literature indicates a different understanding of the Chinese CSR Report Rating. For example, Shen, Wu, and Chand (2017,

p.271) view the CASS-CSRRC as one of the "government-affiliated industry expert assurers" (a type of CSR assurance providers[5]). The Rating is considered a mechanism that adds credibility to CSR reports by "improving their actual and perceived quality" (Shen, Wu, and Chand, 2017, p.275). In this case, the Rating represents a practice performed by "an expert third party" (Shen, Wu, and Chand, 2017, p.275). Similarly, Noronha et al. (2013, p.39) view CASS-CSRRC's Report Rating as "assurance services" for Chinese companies.

Figure 2 shows the process of the Rating. Once a company sets an agreement with the Committee Secretariat, the rating process begins. The Committee randomly selects experts from the expert pool and establishes a rating panel. The panel consists of one leader (an expert), one member (an expert), and several contact persons from the Secretariat.

The Secretariat is responsible for the evaluation of the company's CSR reporting procedures. If this is the first time the company purchases the Rating, a contact person will conduct an online interview with its CSR re-

Figure 2   The process of CSR report rating

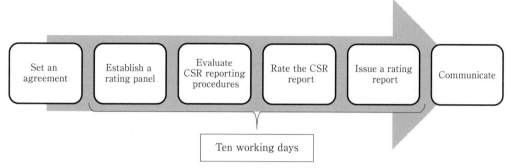

Source: translated and adapted from Chinese Expert Committee on CSR Report Rating (2020, pp.7-8).

porting manager, collect relevant documentary evidence[6], and fill a Procedural Assessment Data Information Confirmation Form[7]. The Form is confirmed and signed by the company. If the company has been continuously involved in the Rating for two or more years, no interview will be conducted. Instead, the contact person will send the Form to the company directly. The company will then fill the form, sign it, and send it with relevant documentary evidence back to the contact person.

After evaluating the reporting procedures, the Secretariat sends the company's CSR report and the Confirmation Form to the rating panel. The rating panel evaluates the CSR report based on CASS-CSR 4.0 (Zhong et al., 2018) and the Chinese Corporate Social Responsibility Report Rating Standards (Chinese Expert Committee on CSR Report Rating, 2020). Notably, the evaluation is based on the text of the CSR report only. The CSR report is then given scores based on seven indicators: Procedure, Substantiality, Integrity, Balance, Comparability, Readability, and Innovation, which account for 20%, 25%, 20%, 10%, 10%, 10%, and 5% of the

overall rating, respectively. The overall rating is determined by the weighted sum of the seven scores, with possible results categorised into seven levels (see Table 1).

Finally, the rating panel leader produces a Rating Report based on the rating scores and the panel members' opinions. The Associate Chairman of the Committee then signs the Rating Report before issuing it. The Secretariat subsequently sends the Rating Report and communicates with the reporting company. The company is expected to include the Rating Report in its CSR report.

The past decade has witnessed the increasing popularity of the CSR Report Rating service. A total number of 597 rating reports have been issued by the end of 2019 (Chinese Expert Committee on CSR Report Rating, 2020). Many Chinese companies, particularly SOEs, invest in the Rating annually. However, the understanding of the Rating is in a muddle. Previous literature (Noronha et al., 2013; Shen, Wu, and Chand, 2017) views the Rating as an alternative (or an equivalent) to CSR assurance, which aims to enhance CSR reports' credibility. However, Chinese Expert Committee on

Table 1   Levels of Rating

Overall rating	Shown as	The level of CSR reporting
Five-star Plus	★★★★★ (+)	Model
Five-star	★★★★★	Outstanding
Four-star and half	★★★★☆	Leading
Four-star	★★★★	Excellent
Three-star	★★★	Good
Two-star	★★	Developing
One-star	★	Beginning

Source: translated and adapted from Chinese Expert Committee on CSR Report Rating (2020, p.15).

CSR Report Rating (2020) indicates that the Rating aims to provide Chinese reporting companies with professional advice and enhance CSR management through better CSR reporting. It implies that the Rating is more like an extension of CSR consulting.

Therefore, the nature and purpose of the Chinese CSR Report Rating are unclear. Moreover, the extant literature remains inconclusive regarding (1) whether the Rating can effectively enhance the credibility of CSR reports and (2) why the Chinese companies, particularly SOEs, prefer the Rating. There is a dearth of qualitative research illuminating the nature, process, and effectiveness of the Rating. Furthermore, there is a lack of engagement-based case studies which provide in-depth insights into the Chinese CSR reporting practice (Adams and Larrinaga, 2019; Li and Belal, 2018; Yang, Craig, and Farley, 2015). This study aims to fill these research gaps. The following chapter summarises the research methods.

3.   Methods

This research examines the nature of the Chinese CSR Report Rating and its effectiveness in enhancing the credibility of CSR reporting. An engagement-based qualitative case study was designed and conducted. The evidence collected for the case study included interview data and documentary evidence.

The approach to interviewee selection involved purposive and self-selection sampling (Saunders, Lewis, and Thornhill, 2019). It was purposive in seeking opinions from CSR reporting managers of the very largest Chinese companies (particularly SOEs), CSR experts from major Chinese CSR consulting firms, and Chinese CSR assurance providers. The sample of ten interviewees included CSR managers/Heads of five large Chinese companies which have adopted the Chinese CSR Report Rating service for years. The sample also included CSR experts from three CSR consulting firms and two CSR assurance providers. Appendix 1 shows the details of the interviewees, with key identity information anonymised.

Table 2   The design of initial interview questions

Interviewee category	Initial interview questions
CSR manager/Head	When did your company start to purchase the CSR Report Rating service? Why did your company purchase the CSR Report Rating service? What value has the CSR Report Rating service provided? How do you perceive the role of CASS-CSRRC in the Chinese CSR field? Is the CSR Report Rating service an alternative to CSR assurance? Could you please compare the CSR Report Rating service and the CSR assurance? Will your company continue purchasing the CSR Report Rating service?
CSR expert	How do you perceive the value the CSR Report Rating service provides? How do you perceive the role of CASS-CSRRC in the Chinese CSR field? Is the CSR Report Rating service an alternative to CSR assurance? Could you please compare the CSR Report Rating service and the CSR assurance? In your opinion, why many companies prefer the CSR Report Rating service? When providing CSR consulting service, will you recommend any mechanism enhancing the credibility of CSR reporting to your clients? What mechanism(s) will you recommend?
CSR assurance provider	Is the CSR Report Rating service an alternative to CSR assurance? Could you please compare the CSR Report Rating service and the CSR assurance? How do you perceive the value the CSR Report Rating service provides? How do you perceive the role of CASS-CSRRC in the Chinese CSR field? In your opinion, why many companies prefer the CSR Report Rating service? In your opinion, why most Chinese companies are reluctant to adopt CSR assurance?

The interviews were semi-structured, where the interviewees were free to speak their minds. Initial interview questions were designed to stimulate reflection, which sought to capture the interviewees' views on (1) the driving forces behind adopting the Rating; and (2) the effectiveness of the Rating. Table 2 shows the design of the initial interview questions.

Follow-up questions captured insights into the relationships between the elements being considered. The interviews were conducted during 2019, which yielded 10.9 hours of audio recordings. The recordings were transcribed verbatim, with transcriptions being checked by the researcher.

A thematic analysis of the interview data was then conducted. The analytical procedure involved four elements: (1) becoming familiar with the interview data, (2) coding the interview data, (3) searching for themes and recognising relationships, (4) refining themes and testing propositions (Saunders, Lewis, and Thornhill, 2019). Notably, this procedure did not occur in a simple linear progression but concurrently and recurrently. The analysis of a series of documents (see Appendix 2) supplemented the thematic analysis of the interview data. Five main themes were identified from the data analysis, namely "drivers", "purpose", "process", "nature", and "effectiveness".

4. Findings

The analysis findings reveal the symbolic nature of the Chinese CSR Report Rating, which is reflected in three aspects. First, the Rating features heavy governmental influence. The evidence reveals that SOEs account for most of the client base in the Rating service and prefer the service because CASS-CSRRC is a government-affiliated research institution:

"The CSR Report Rating is considered authoritative. Companies, including Central Enterprises, other SOEs, private companies, and foreign companies, all recognise it. Therefore, we also use it," (MAN-1).

MAN-1 and MAN-5 further noted that by cooperating with CASS-CSRRC, they could maintain a good relationship with the central government and gain access to critical resources controlled by the state. As MAN-5 put it:

"[CASS-CSRRC] has an official and authoritative background ... It has a close relationship with our superior regulatory authority, SASAC. Through [cooperating with] CASS-CSRRC, we can be tied up with our superior in some projects," (MAN-5).

The evidence indicates that the Rating serves the companies' strategy to gain political legitimacy[8] (Marquis and Qian, 2014; Zhao, 2012). SOEs have significant political responsibilities and are required to work as political actors (Zhu and Zhang, 2015), and therefore have a strong desire to appear more legitimate. They cooperate with CASS-CSRRC and adopt the Rating to meet the state's social and environmental expectations, obtain and retain policy legitimacy, and gain state resources (Marquis and Qian, 2014; Zhao, 2012). Moreover, AP-2 implied that reporting companies would always get a satisfying result from the Rating, with their CSR reports rated as "Leading" or "Out-

standing". Hence, the Rating is primarily a political legitimacy tool used by the Chinese CSR reporting companies, especially SOEs.

Second, the purpose of the CSR Report Rating is ambiguous. The reporting companies tend to view the Rating as a credibility-enhancing mechanism. MAN-1, MAN-2, MAN-3, MAN-4, and MAN-5 broadly agreed that the Rating represented opinions from an authoritative and independent research institution (CASS-CSRRC). A Rating Report issued by CASS-CSRRC meant that the CSR report was endorsed by an authoritative and "neutral third party" (MAN-2). MAN-2 further noted that "in the absence of CSR assurance, the Rating largely represents the credibility [of CSR reporting], just like [what] the assurance [can provide]". However, other interviewees (EXP-1, EXP-2, EXP-3, AP-1, AP-2) noted that the Rating should not be considered equivalent to CSR assurance. The following quotes elaborate:

"CSR assurance merely [focuses on data] reliability ... The Rating does not assess the data reliability ... It evaluates whether a company has fully disclosed the CSR information as required" (EXP-1).

"[CASS-CSRRC] can provide [the Rating service] ... but I think it is not assurance ... if the Rating could replace the assurance, the assurance would not exist ... they are essentially incomparable" (AP-2).

Notably, AP-1 pointed out that CASS-CSRRC should not be regarded as an assurance provider or external reviewer due to its lack of independence:

"CASS-CSRRC helps companies write CSR

reports and then rates them. Consequently, the credibility [of the Rating] loses ... That is why CASS-CSRRC has been despised [by peers] in this industry" (AP-1).

MAN-1, MAN-2, and MAN-5 indicated that CASS-CSRRC provided consulting, report writing, and report rating services for them simultaneously, with the Rating as part of the CSR consulting service contract. As MAN-2 put it:

"[CASS-CSRRC] is both an authoritative rating organisation and a consultant, or think tank, that can provide advice regarding CSR strategy. Also, it cooperates with the government. Hence, for us, it has a comprehensive role," (MAN-2).

The evidence reveals that the Rating is in fact an extension or a "variant" of CSR consulting but broadly considered equivalent to CSR assurance aiming at credibility-enhancing. However, the fact that CASS-CSRRC rates its own work threatens its independence as an external reviewer. The lack of independence seriously undermines the commonly expected effectiveness of the Rating in credibility-enhancing.

Third, the process of the CSR Report Rating is also questionable. The report evaluation is "based on the text only, without checking the accuracy of CSR data disclosed" (EXP-1). AP-1 further noted the lack of procedures such as site visit and staff enquiry, pointing to an absence of stakeholder engagement during the rating process:

"[CASS-CSRRC] does not conduct a site visit but only asks the companies to send electronic CSR reports. Then the rating panel can is-

sue rating reports ... [this rating process] lacks stakeholder engagement as it is based on the text only" (AP-1).

The evidence indicates that the rating process is oversimplified, completely ignoring data accuracy and stakeholder engagement. Therefore, the evaluation of CSR reporting quality is superficial, further undermining the effectiveness of the CSR Report Rating in credibility-enhancing.

The discussion above indicates that the nature of the CSR Report Rating is symbolic, which is reflected in three aspects. First, the CSR Report Rating is essentially a tool that the companies, especially SOEs, use as part of their CSR strategy to gain political legitimacy and access to state resources. With their CSR reports rated as "Outstanding" or "Leading", the companies can show their achievement in CSR performance and thus meet the state's social and environmental expectations. Therefore, the CSR Report Rating is more like "a promotional tool of business image" (Noronha et al., 2013, p. 39) rather than an unbiased evaluation of CSR reporting quality.

Second, the symbolic nature of the Rating is further revealed due to the ambiguity about its purpose. The main doubt is whether the Rating is an extension of CSR consulting or an alternative to CSR assurance. The CSR reporting managers interviewed (MAN-1, MAN-2, MAN-3, MAN-4, and MAN-5) were broadly in agreement that the Rating could function as CSR assurance and enhance the credibility of CSR reporting. However, CASS-CSRRC's lack of independence as an external reviewer/assurance provider seriously undermines the effectiveness of the Rating in credibility-enhancing. The fact that CASS-CSRRC reviews the reports prepared by itself reveals that the CSR Report Rating is largely a self-review practice with symbolic nature.

Third, the Rating process is superficial. The Rating is based on the text of CSR reports only, without checking data accuracy and engaging key stakeholders. This finding means that a CSR report can still gain a high rate/ score even if the data disclosed is incorrect or manipulated. Therefore, the oversimplified rating process further points to the symbolic nature of the CSR Report Rating practice.

Overall, the symbolic nature of the CSR Report Rating indicates that its effectiveness in credibility- enhancing is questionable. The Rating is more like an extension or a "variant" of CSR consulting, a mechanism for companies' CSR strategy, and a business image enhancement tool, rather than an alternative to CSR assurance.

5. | Conclusion

The purpose of this paper is to examine and explain the nature of the CSR Report Rating, a CSR-related practice developed and provided by CASS-CSRRC in China. An engagement-based case study has been conducted in response to the lack of qualitative evidence within the extant literature illuminating the nature and effectiveness of the Rating. The evidence collected for the case study combined interview data and a series of relevant documents. The case study analysis reveals three key findings pointing to the symbolic

nature of the CSR Report Rating:

   (1) the CSR Report Rating is typically used as a political legitimacy tool;

   (2) the CSR Report Rating is largely a self-review practice; and

   (3) the rating process is oversimplified and superficial.

In summary, the CSR Report Rating's effectiveness in enhancing the credibility of CSR reports is questionable. It should not be regarded as an alternative (or an equivalent) to CSR assurance.

This case study makes several contributions to CSR accounting and reporting research. Firstly, this study represents an early attempt to investigate the Chinese CSR Report Rating practice under-researched within the extant literature. Further, as a response to the call for more engagement research (Adams and Larrinaga, 2019), this study provides qualitative evidence through fieldwork-based research on the development of CSR reporting practice in China, the world's largest emerging economy.

Secondly, this study contributes to a comprehensive and nuanced understanding of the CSR Report Rating. In both practice and academia, the current understanding is in a muddle, with ambiguity about its purpose and nature. This paper clears up the ambiguity by suggesting that the CSR Report Rating is more like an extension or a "variant" of CSR consulting rather than an alternative to CSR assurance. Therefore, the CSR Report Rating should not be viewed as a credibility-enhancing mechanism.

Finally, this study has important practical implications. The symbolic nature of the CSR Report Rating implies that the nature of Chinese CSR reports can also be symbolic. Chinese CSR reports are typically used as a legitimation or corporate image enhancement tool, rather than a genuine accountability medium for stakeholders and the wider public (Lee, Walker, and Zeng, 2017; Marquis and Qian, 2014; Patten, Ren, and Zhao, 2015; Zhao and Pattern, 2016). This research further implies that the CSR reports' credibility is doubtful. Hence, there is an urgent demand for credibility-enhancing mechanisms for Chinese CSR reporting. For example, regulators and policymakers may consider requiring independent external assurance for CSR reporting to ensure the completeness and reliability of CSR disclosures.

This qualitative case study is inevitably subject to some limitations. While the interviews allowed access to the managers involved in the preparation of CSR reports, the practitioners in the CSR consulting and assurance market, and some internal documents, the researcher was only given access to information and organisational documents that were not confidential. Therefore, the empirical analysis is mainly based on the interviewee' reflections. Moreover, the CSR reporting managers interviewed were mainly from the very largest SOEs. Hence, the generalisation of the key findings of this exploratory study might be restricted.

Future research could explore the CSR reporting practice of SOEs (either at the central or local level), foreign companies, or private companies operating in China. Particularly, the investigation of foreign and private companies would be interesting due to their location in a unique socioeconomic, political, and cultural context (Li and Belal, 2018). Furthermore, while this study has focused on the Chinese CSR Report Rating, future research could go further and explore other CSR-related practices in China. For example, the CSR assurance practice in China is a topic currently under-researched. Research on this topic can provide empirical insights for policymakers who can assist the development of regulations for CSR reporting and assurance.

(1)　The State-owned Assets Supervision and Administration Commission of the State Council (SASAC) is a ministry directly under the management of the State Council (SASAC, 2021a).

(2)　Central Enterprises are also referred to as Central State-owned Enterprises. They are wholly or partly owned and directed by the Central Government or government ministries such as the Ministry of Finance and SASAC (SASAC, 2021b).

(3)　CSR/sustainability assurance is defined as assurance on CSR/sustainability reports (Canning, O'Dwyer, and Georgakopoulos, 2019). Assurance is defined as "an engagement in which a practitioner aims to obtain sufficient appropriate evidence in order to express a conclusion designed to enhance the degree of confidence of the intended users other than the responsible party about the subject matter information" (IAASB, 2013, p.7). CSR assurance is expected to enhance the credibility of CSR reports and assist better decision making (Shen, Wu, and Chand, 2017).

(4)　The Chinese Academy of Social Sciences (CASS) is an academic organisation and comprehensive research centre of the People's Republic of China in philosophy and social sciences (CASS, 2021).

(5)　CSR assurance providers are typically categorised into accounting assurance providers and non-accounting assurance providers (see, for example, Bepari and Mollik, 2016; Boiral and Heras-Saizarbitoria, 2020; Channuntapipat, Samsonova-Taddei, and Turley, 2020; Farooq and De Villiers, 2017; 2019; Gürtürk and Hahn, 2016). Shen, Wu, and Chand (2017) have added another categorise of CSR assurance providers in the Chinese context, which is called "industry expert assurers" (p. 274).

(6)　According to Chinese Expert Committee on CSR Report Rating (2020, p. 9), the documentary evidence includes, but is not limited to, the company's internal written record of (1) CSR reporting team members and respective responsibilities, (2) staff training on CSR reporting, (3) stakeholders, the process of stakeholder engagement, and stakeholder feedback, (4) the process of materiality assessment, (5) the process of report writing.

(7)　For details of the Procedural Assessment Data Information Confirmation Form, please see Chinese Expert Committee on CSR Report Rating (2020, pp. 20–21).

(8)　Political legitimacy is defined as "the extent to which the government views the firm's actions as being in accordance with norms and laws" (Marquis and Qian, 2014, p. 127).

Appendices

Appendix 1   Details of Interview Data Collection

Interview Code	Organisa-tion Code	Organisation Type	Sector	Interviewee Code	Position	Interview Duration (In minute)
1	FIRM-1	SOE	Energy	MAN-1	Manager of CSR reporting, Publicity Department	90
2	FIRM-2	SOE	Energy	MAN-2	Manger of CSR reporting, CSR Office	96
3	FIRM-3	SOE	Engineering and Construction	MAN-3	Head of CSR reporting, Corporate Culture (Party Work) Department	52
4	FIRM-4	Non-SOE	Food Production	MAN-4	Manager of CSR reporting, Group General Affair Department	85
5	FIRM-5	SOE	Motor Vehicles and Parts	MAN-5	Head of Corporate Responsi-bility, Brand Promotion Office, Party Work Department	46
6	CON-1	CSR Consulting firm	Professional Service	EXP-1	Associate Head	38
7	CON-2	CSR Consulting firm	Professional Service	EXP-2	Director, Chief Executive Officer (CEO) and Co-founder	72
8	CON-3	CSR Consulting firm	Professional Services	EXP-3	CSR Consulting Director	63
9	AP-1	Technical Service Provider (Non-accounting CSR assurance provider)	Professional Services	SAP-1	Assurance Project Manager	41
10	AP-2	Big Four accounting firm (Accounting CSR assurance provider)	Professional Services	SAP-2	Senior Manager	72
Total						655

Appendix 2   Details of Documentary Evidence

Document Type	Details
Standards	*The Chinese Corporate Social Responsibility Report Rating Standards* (Chinese Expert Committee on CSR Report Rating, 2020)
Rating reports	Sample companies' every rating report published from the earliest available to the latest one (the year 2019)
CSR reports	Sample companies' every CSR report from the earliest available to the latest one (the year 2019)
Company websites	Accessed several times between 2019 and 2020. Details of the websites cannot be provided due to confidentiality reasons.
Other relevant documents	Internal documents provided by some interviewees

〈References〉

Adams, C. A. and Larrinaga, C. (2019) 'Progress: Engaging with Organisations in Pursuit of Improved Sustainability Accounting and Performance,' *Accounting, Auditing and Accountability Journal*, Vol. 32, No. 8, pp. 2367–2394.

Bepari, M. K. and Mollik, A. T. (2016) "Stakeholders' Interest in Sustainability Assurance Process,' *Managerial Auditing Journal*, Vol. 31, No. 6/7, pp. 655–687.

Boiral, O. and Heras-Saizarbitoria, I. (2020) 'Sustainability Reporting Assurance: Creating Stakeholder Accountability through Hyperreality?,' *Journal of Cleaner Production*, Vol. 243, pp. 1–17.

Canning, M., O'Dwyer, B. and Georgakopoulos, G. (2019) 'Processes of Auditability in Sustainability Assurance – The Case of Materiality Construction,' *Accounting and Business Research*, Vol. 49, No. 1, pp. 1–27.

CASS (2021) About CASS, Available at http://casseng. cssn.cn/about/about_cass/, Accessed April 23rd 2021.

Channuntapipat, C., Samsonova-Taddei, A. and Turley, S. (2020) 'Variation in Sustainability Assurance Practice: An Analysis of Accounting versus Non-accounting Providers,' *The British Accounting Review*, Vol. 52, No. 2, pp. 1–17.

Chinese Expert Committee on CSR Report Rating (2020) The Chinese Corporate Social Responsibility Report Rating Standards, Available at https:// ncstatic.clewm.net/rsrc/2020/0309/11/e2fc9a6ca3f 20dce0cf0693339a00dd4.pdf, Accessed April 23rd 2021.

Farooq, M. B. and De Villiers, C. (2017) 'The Market for Sustainability Assurance Services', *Pacific Accounting Review*, Vol. 29, No. 1, pp. 79–106.

―― M. B. and De Villiers, C. (2019) 'The Shaping of Sustainability Assurance through the Competition between Accounting and Non-accounting Providers,' *Accounting, Auditing and Accountability Journal*, Vol. 32, No. 1, pp. 307–336.

Global Reporting Initiative (GRI) (2016) GRI 101: Foundation, Amsterdam.

Gürtürk, A. and Hahn, R. (2016) 'An Empirical Assessment of Assurance Statements in Sustainability Reports: Smoke Screens or Enlightening Information?,' *Journal of Cleaner Production*, No. 136, pp. 30–41.

International Auditing and Assurance Standards Broad

(IAASB) (2013) *ISAE 3000 (Revised), Assurance Engagements Other than Audits or Reviews of Historical Financial Information*, New York: International Federation of Accountants.

KPMG (2011) International Survey of Corporate Responsibility Reporting 2011, Available at http://www. kpmg.com/au/en/issuesandinsights/articlespubli cations/pages/corporateresponsibility-reporting-survey-2011.aspx, Accessed April 23rd 2021.

―― (2020) The Time Has Come: The KPMG Survey of Sustainability Reporting 2020, Available at https://home.kpmg/xx/en/home/insights/2020/ 11/the-time-has-come-survey-of-sustainability-reporting.html, Accessed April 23rd 2021.

Laufer, W. S. (2003) 'Social Accountability and Corporate Greenwashing,' *Journal of Business Ethics*, Vol. 43, No. 3, pp. 253–261.

Lee, E., Walker, M. and Zeng, C. C. (2017) 'Do Chinese State Subsidies Affect Voluntary Corporate Social Responsibility Disclosure?,' *Journal of Accounting and Public Policy*, Vol. 36, No. 3, pp. 179–200.

Li, T. and Belal, A. (2018) 'Authoritarian State, Global Expansion and Corporate Social Responsibility Reporting: The Narrative of a Chinese State-owned Enterprise,' *Accounting Forum*, Vol. 42, No. 2, pp. 199–217.

Mahoney, L. S., Thorne, L., Cecil, L. and LaGore, W. (2013) 'A Research Note on Standalone Corporate Social Responsibility Reports: Signalling or Greenwashing?,' *Critical Perspectives on Accounting*, Vol. 24, No. 4–5, pp. 350–359.

Marquis, C. and Qian, C. (2014) 'Corporate Social Responsibility Reporting in China: Symbol or Substance?,' *Organization Science*, Vol. 25, No. 1, pp. 127–148.

Noronha, C., Tou, S., Cynthia, M. I. and Guan, J. J. (2013) 'Corporate Social Responsibility Reporting in China: An Overview and Comparison with Major Trends,' *Corporate Social Responsibility and Environmental Management*, Vol. 20, No. 1, pp. 29–42.

Patten, D. M., Ren, Y. and Zhao, N. (2015) 'Standalone Corporate Social Responsibility Reporting in China: An Exploratory Analysis of its Relation to Legitimation,' *Social and Environmental Accountability Journal*, Vol. 35, No. 1, pp. 17–31.

SASAC (2008) Recommendations for Central Enterprises on Fulfilling Social Responsibility. Available at http://www.gov.cn/zwgk/2008-01/04/content_ 850589.htm, Accessed April 23rd 2021.

—— (2021a) Directory, Available at http://en.sasac.gov.cn/directory.html, Accessed April 23rd 2021.

—— (2021b) About Us, Available at http://en.sasac.gov.cn/2018/07/17/c_7.htm, Accessed 23rd April 2021.

Saunders, M. N., Lewis, P. and Thornhill, A. (2019) *Research Methods for Business Students (8th edn)*, New York: Pearson Education.

Shabana, K. M., Buchholtz, A. K. and Carroll, A. B. (2017) 'The institutionalisation of corporate social responsibility reporting,' *Business & Society*, Vol. 56, No. 8, pp. 1107–1135.

Shen, H., Wu, H. and Chand, P. (2017) 'The Impact of Corporate Social Responsibility Assurance on Investor Decisions: Chinese Evidence,' *International Journal of Auditing*, Vol. 21, No. 3, pp. 271–287.

Simnett, R., Zhou, S. and Hoang, H. (2016) 'Assurance and Other Credibility Enhancing Mechanisms for Integrated Reporting', in Mio C. (Ed.), *Integrated Reporting*, pp. 269–286, London: Palgrave Macmillan.

Uyar, A., Karaman, A. S. and Kilic, M. (2020) 'Is Corporate Social Responsibility Reporting a Tool of Signalling or Greenwashing? Evidence from the Worldwide Logistics Sector,' *Journal of Cleaner Production*, Vol. 253, pp. 1–13.

Yang, H. H., Craig, R. and Farley, A. (2015) 'A Review of Chinese and English Language Studies on Corporate Environmental Reporting in China,' *Critical Perspectives on Accounting*, Vol. 28, pp. 30–48.

Yin, G., Guan, Z., Jia, L., Li, R. and Quan S. (2019) 'The Research on Corporate Social Responsibility Reporting in China,' in Goldenbee Research on Corporate Social Responsibility Reporting in China (2019) (pp. 1–67). Social Sciences Academic Press (China).

Zhao, M. (2012) 'CSR-based Political Legitimacy Strategy: Managing the State by Doing Good in China and Russia,' *Journal of Business Ethics*, Vol. 111, No. 4, pp. 439–460.

Zhao, N. and Patten, D. M. (2016) 'An Exploratory Analysis of Managerial Perceptions of Social and Environmental Reporting in China: Evidence from State-owned Enterprises in Beijing,' *Sustainability Accounting, Management and Policy Journal*, Vol. 7, No. 1, pp. 80–98.

Zhong, H., Wang, J., Zhang E., and Lei, S. (2018) The Chinese Corporate Social Responsibility Reporting Guide (CASS-CSR 4.0), Beijing: Economy and Management Publishing House.

Zhu, Q. and Zhang, Q. (2015) 'Evaluating Practices and Drivers of Corporate Social Responsibility: The Chinese Context,' *Journal of Cleaner Production*, Vol. 100, pp. 315–324.

——, Liu, J., and Lai, K. H. (2016) 'Corporate Social Responsibility Practices and Performance Improvement Among Chinese National State-owned Enterprises,' *International Journal of production economics*, Vol. 171, pp. 417–426.

56　企業と社会フォーラム学会誌，第 10 号，pp. 56-61，2021

インクルーシブ・グロース（IG）は
企業の経営戦略として有効なのか
——インド・ドリシュティ社を中心として

足立　伸也

法政大学大学院公共政策研究科博士後期課程

キーワード：インクルーシブ・グロース（IG），IG4 原則，IG 戦略，インド農村，ドリシュティ社，エコシステム，農村起業家

【要旨】

　「インクルーシブ（包摂的／包括的）・グロース（成長）（Inclusive Growth：IG）」という概念は，国際開発の文脈から誕生した。アジア開発銀行，世界銀行の文書に IG という用語が使用されるようになり，それ以降，国際開発や各国政策において IG が重視されるようになった。

　また，IG を企業戦略として活用する動きも進み，Kaplan et al.（2018; 2019）は企業の IG 戦略実現のための 4 つの原則（IG4 原則）を提唱した。本事例紹介では，インド農村にてビジネスを展開するドリシュティ社に IG4 原則を当てはめ，同社の IG 戦略を考察した。ドリシュティ社の例では，進出先の農村起業家がパートナーとしてエコシステムに参画することで企業と農村との信頼関係が育まれ，その信頼関係がエコシステムに多くの組織・団体・個人が集う環境に繋がっていた。このような結果から IG 戦略は，地元人材を巻き込むエコシステムが有効であると考えられる。

1. はじめに

　「インクルーシブ（包摂的／包括的）・グロース（成長）（Inclusive Growth：IG）」という概念は国際開発の分野から誕生した。IG の用語が文書に登場し始めたのは，Ali（2007），Ianchovichina and Lundstrom（2009）などアジア開発銀行，世界銀行の文書であり，途上国のより脆弱な人々を取り残さないという国際開発の方向性を示してきた。一方，同時期からインド，フィリピンなどアジア各国を中心に国家政策として IG が使用されている。

　2010 年代以降，IG は，企業の経営戦略としても重視されている。Deloitte（2018）は，「IG は顧客の信頼や人材の管理・維持といった重要課題よりも大きな課題として認識されており，経営者の関心事として IG よりも唯一高い地位を占めたのは，技術競争力へのキャッチアップのみであった」と述べている。また Kaplan et al.（2018; 2019）は，企業が IG を実現していくための 4 つの原則（以下，IG4 原則）を提唱し

投稿（事例紹介・解説）（2021. 2. 18 受付 / 2021. 5. 16 受理）

表 1　現地調査概要

表 1　現地調査概要

調査時期	調査州	主な調査項目	調査人数
2015 年 3 月 12〜14 日	ウッタル・プラデーシュ州	創業経緯 現在までのストーリー 本社と支店の関係性 支店のビジネス 農村起業家のビジネス	ノイダ本社経営幹部 2 名，本社社員 1 名（人事担当），マトゥーラ支店 2 名（責任者・社員），農村起業家 4 名（パソコン教室オーナー 2 名，農村キオスクオーナー 2 名），パソコン教室生徒 8 名，農村キオスク顧客 1 名
2015 年 9 月 21〜23 日	ウッタル・プラデーシュ州	各社の連携度合い ドリシュティ社の課題 社会性と経済性のバランス	ノイダ本社経営幹部 7 名（共同創業者他各ビジネスの責任者）
2015 年 9 月 24〜26 日	ビハール州	農村ビジネスの実態 農村住民のドリシュティ社への反応 インターンの役割	マドゥバニ支店 2 名（責任者・社員），職業教育先生 2 名（農業・英語各 1 名），ソーラス村農村起業家 1 名（女性ショップオーナー），学生インターン 2 名

出所：筆者作成。

た。IG4 原則は，次の通りである。

(1) エコシステムへの参加者に関わる事業機会を探すこと
(2) 補完的パートナーを動員すること
(3) 事業化や規模拡大のための資金を獲得すること
(4) 新たなエコシステム関係者との戦略共有とモニタリングシステムを導入すること

　Kaplan et al.（2018）は，IG を「持続可能なエコシステムに参加するすべての組織・団体が恩恵を受ける成長」と定義し，IG4 原則をもとに「包括的で持続的かつ収益性も高いエコシステムを生み出すことができる戦略を策定することが必要である」と述べている。

　しかし，社会実装化に向けて，IG4 原則をもとにした事例分析などによる研究・調査は十分でない。そこで，本稿では，インドのドリシュティ社を事例に，Anu Singh Lather et al.（2009），加藤（2011），佐野ら（2012），Desa and Koch（2015）の先行研究も踏まえながら，IG が企業の経営戦略になり得るかを考察する。な

お，筆者は同社関係者への半構造化インタビューを中心に，現地調査を実施した（表 1 参照）。

2.　事例紹介　ドリシュティ社

　インド政府は，2014 年 4 月に世界で初めて CSR 法「The Companies Act 2013」[1] を施行し，貧困を含むさまざまな社会問題解決にビジネスを積極的に活用している。ドリシュティ社は創業以来，インド全 28 州のうち 10 州 5,000 以上の農村でビジネスを展開し，15,000 人以上の農村起業家創出実績がある。その社会性の高さやビジネスモデルの革新性などから国内外で高い評価を得ている[2]。

　同社は 2000 年に「Drishtee Development And Communication Ltd（DDCL）」として創業し，以後，「Drishtee Foundation（DF）」，「Drishtee Skill Development Center Private Ltd（DSDC）」と別組織を立ち上げ，各組織の役割分担を明確にしている[3]。特に「DF」は非営利財団であるため，インドの税法上寄付や出資が 100％非課税となる[4]。その税制優遇も踏まえ，国内外企業・団体は「DF」と連携を進める。「DF」

表2　ドリシュティ社3組織の損益計算書（抜粋）

	DDCL		DF		DSDC	
正式名称	Drishtee Development And Communication Ltd		Drishtee Foundation		Drishtee Skill Development Center Private Ltd	
設立年	2000 年		2003 年		2012 年	
従業員数	150 名		70 名		60 名　別講師 100 名	
事業内容	農村起業家, 住民への商品・サービス提供		農村住民, 団体・企業との連携		農村住民への職業教育実施	
会計年	(2015.3.31)	(2014.3.31)	(2015.3.31)	(2014.3.31)	(2015.3.31)	(2014.3.31)
総収入	93,944	90,677	56,293	74,257	29,803	11,980
総支出	87,823	87,894	52,541	69,530	42,140	21,855
管理費・その他経費	48,348	43,743	11,033	14,140	19,211	9,949
税引き前当期純利益	6,121	2,762	3,752	4,727	▲ 12,337	▲ 9,874
当期純利益	6,865	2,236	3,752	4,727	▲ 8,683	▲ 6,864

※単位は千ルピー［1 ルピー =1.41 円（2020 年 12 月 14 日）外務省］，▲は赤字を示す。
出所：各組織が発行する非公開の損益計算書に基づき筆者作成。

の財務情報[5]によると，多国籍企業や社会的財団などの 10 以上のプロジェクトがあり，その収入は「DF」収入の 88％にも及ぶ。例えば，日本のリコーとのプロジェクトである「Rangoli ショップ」は，女性オーナーによる女性向けキオスクのコンセプトが受け入れられ，2011 年 11 月に 1 店舗目が開店，40 店舗以上に拡大している[6]。3 組織の損益計算書の抜粋を分析[7]すると，2015 年 3 月時点において，「DSDC」の赤字を「DDCL」と「DF」が補い，ドリシュティ社として 193.4 万ルピー（約 272.7 万円）の黒字であることが分かる（表 2 参照）。

同社の資料によると，ビジネス展開先の中規模農村の実態は，1 日のうち電気が使える時間は 4 時間，銀行口座開設率 10％，1 ヵ月の世帯平均月収 2,750 ルピーなどである。このような農村に対して，同社は前身の IT 企業としての強み，システムやネットワークなどのデジタル技術も駆使しながら，農村起業家を介した住民への多品種の商品・サービス提供ビジネスを展開している。具体的なビジネスとして，農村住民に対する金融サービス，職業教育，日用品配送，農業支援などがあり，国内外企業や政府・

図1　ドリシュティ社のビジネスモデル

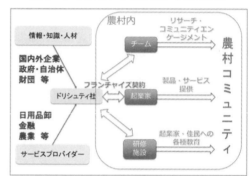

出所：ドリシュティ社公開情報，ならびにビハール州マトゥバニ支店幹部とのヒアリング等を基に筆者作成。

自治体，財団などがそれらのビジネスを支えるパートナーとして参画している（図1参照）。同社が農村ビジネスエコシステムの中心となり，農村内外の多様な組織や人と繋がることで，農村コミュニティを形成・維持している。

3.　事例考察　ドリシュティ社の IG

同社のビジネスは，Kaplan et al. (2018) が提示した IG4 原則に当てはめると表のように整理できる（表3参照）。同社は，ビジネスを通じてインド農村の問題解決を行い，表2の損

表3　IG4原則とドリシュティ社の事例

IG4原則	事例
(1) エコシステムへの参加者に関わる事業機会を探すこと	農村住民のニーズを自身も住民である農村起業家が，ドリシュティ社のパートナーとして解決する。
(2) 補完的パートナーを動員すること	公的機関（政府・自治体），民間企業，研究者，インターン，ボランティアを募り，参入余地を広げる。
(3) 事業化や規模拡大のための資金を獲得すること	公的機関からの事業委託，複数の社会的投資財団からの資金提供により組織規模を大きくする。
(4) 新たなエコシステム関係者との戦略共有とモニタリングシステムを導入すること	ドリシュティ社員が農村起業家を都度支援する。農村内での暗黙モニタリングシステムを活用する。

出所：ドリシュティ社先行研究，現地調査，関係者ヒアリングなどを踏まえて筆者作成。

益計算書の通り，事業性も担保している。同社は，農村住民である農村起業家とも連携し，また，農村住民から社員を募集し，社員として雇用する。そのことで，同社のビジネスが農村に受け入れられやすい環境を整え，農村や住民の実態を踏まえた商品・サービス提供を通じて農村住民のニーズを満たす。公的機関（政府・自治体）は，住民へのサービス補完の点から委託などを通じて同社のビジネスを支援し，民間企業は農村への事業開発の機会として参画する。社会的投資財団の一つアキュメンファンドも160万ドルを投資し，同社のビジネスを応援している[8]。他方，同社は，農村起業家や農村社員と既存顧客・潜在顧客である住民との人間関係を基にした，モニタリングシステムを有している。このモニタリングシステムによって，住民から率直なフィードバックが得られ，商品・サービスの改善に繋がる。

　一方，同社には課題も存在する。それは組織の持続性の不確かさである。同社は事業として利益も上げ定性的な面も含めて，「持続可能なエコシステムに参加するすべての組織・団体が恩恵を受ける成長」ではある。実際に同社は，事業性が見込めないテーマのビジネスは実施しない。例えばヘルスケアサービスの不足は農村の課題の一つであるが，政府の規制，医師・看護師の採用が困難である点からサービス実施に

は至っていない。また，想定した収益が上げられなければ，事業継続を断念する[9]。しかし，特に事業性からそのエコシステムの持続性が高められるかは心許ない。同社の経営層は揃って「農村への良い影響が第一で収益性はその次である」とビジネスの社会性を強調する[10]。COO（最高執行責任者）のグプタ氏は，「商品の仕入れ値，売値は本部が決め，個々の農村起業家は利益を上げ，起業家の生計向上に寄与しているが，当社としては利益確保に課題がある」と事業性追求の苦労を吐露している。

　最後に，同社の事例をKaplan et al.（2018）が述べている「包括的で持続的かつ収益性も高いエコシステムを生み出すことができる戦略」と照らし合わせて確認する。包括性は，農村に関わる多様な関係者の巻き込みという点からあると判断できる。持続性は，2000年の創業以来，会社が継続している点からあると判断できる。収益性は，表2の損益計算書の通り，一定程度あると判断できる。この結果から，事業性に改善の余地はあるものの，同社の事例はIG4原則にも当てはまり，IG戦略に合致しているといえる。

4.　おわりに

　本稿は，Kaplan et al.（2018; 2019）のIG4原

則を踏まえ，企業の IG 戦略を考察した。ドリシュティ社の事例を通して，農村人材を活用し，ビジネス関係者がエコシステムに持続的に関わる動機を有する仕組みがあれば，IG は有効性がある点を示した。企業は経営戦略の一つとして，進出先の地元人材を活用した持続的エコシステムの形成を戦略に落とし込める可能性がある。その際には，エコシステムへの参画しやすさと組織の持続性の観点から事業性に留意した仕組みをバランスさせるべきである。

　本稿では，資料の制約から組織や事業別の収益性分析ができなかったが，「インド農村での IG」という点から「途上国の農村ビジネス」や「企業のサステナビリティ」研究の一助になると考えられる。今後，ドリシュティ社の動向や資料を継続的に確認し，追跡調査を試みるのと同時に，他国農村ビジネスを展開する企業にも IG 戦略が有効か検証を重ねたい。

(1)　インドの CSR 法は大企業が直近 3ヵ年の純利益の 2% 平均を CSR 活動に充てるというものである。Varottil（2018）は論文「インド会社法の下での CSR 支出要件分析」で CSR 法の成立過程を含む詳細を分析している。

(2)　ドリシュティ社 Website（2021）より。「最もアジア太平洋地域で成長の早い企業 50 社（デロイト社）」選出，「クリントン・イニシアティブ」へ招聘，世界銀行，アショカ財団，シュワブ財団からの社会企業家賞受賞などがある。

(3)　各組織の経営幹部は重複し，各従業員の認識も個別組織名でなく，Drishtee である点を現地で確認した。

(4)　Council on Foundations（2020）より。

(5)　ドリシュティ社非公開資料「DRISHTEE FOUNDATION BALANCE SHEET AS ON MARCH 31, 2015」より。

(6)　CSO ネットワーク（2014）や日本経済新聞（2013）に背景を含めた詳細情報がある。

(7)　ドリシュティ社非公開資料下記 3 点より。
　・「DRISHTEE DEVELOPMENT & COMMUNICATION LIMITED BALANCE SHEET AS ON 31 ST, MARCH 2015」
　・「DRISHTEE FOUNDATION BALANCE SHEET AS ON MARCH 31, 2015」
　・「DRISHTEE SKILL DEVELOPMENT CENTER PRIVATE LIMITED BALANCE SHEET AS ON 31 ST, MARCH, 2015」

(8)　Chanchani（2008）REUTERS 記事「アキュメンファンド 2 つのエネルギーコストへの 226 万ドル投資」より。

(9)　例えば，ビハール州マトゥバニ支店ソーラス村での日用品卸事業は，想定した収益が上がらず，2010 年に撤退した。

(10)　筆者が 2015 年 9 月に実施した CEO シッダールタ氏とのヒアリングより。例えば，インド農村ではくじの人気があり，流通させれば儲かるそうだが，農村に悪影響を与えるためドリシュティ社はくじを扱っていない。

〈参考文献〉

Ali, I. (2007) *Pro-Poor to Inclusive Growth: Asian Prescriptions*, Manila: Asian Development Bank.

Anand, R., Tulin, V. and Kumar, N. (2014) *India: Defining and Explaining Inclusive Growth and Poverty Reduction*, Washington: International Monetary Fund.

Chanchani, M. A. (2008) 'Acumen fund invests $2.26 mn in two energy cos,' Available at https://www.reuters.com/article/idINIndia-36364820081106, Accessed February 14th 2021.

Council on Foundations (2020) 'NONPROFIT LAW IN INDIA,' Available at https://www.cof.org/content/nonprofit-law-india#Types, Accessed February 14th 2021.

CSO ネットワーク（2014）「グローバル企業は途上国の社会課題にどう取り組んでいるか？」。Available at https://www.csonj.org/images/csonj_booklet003.pdf, Accessed February 14th 2021.

Deloitte Touche Tohmatsu Limited (2018) *The business case for inclusive growth: Deloitte Global inclusive growth survey.*（デロイト トーマツ コンサルティング合同会社訳『Inclusive growth に向けた経営戦略，デロイト トーマツ コンサルティング合同会社，2018 年）

De Mello, L. and Dutz, M. A. (eds.) (2012) *Promoting Inclusive Growth: Challenges and Policies*, Paris: OECD Publishing.

Desa, G. and Koch, J. L. (2015) 'Drishtee: Balancing social mission and financial sustainability in rural India,' *The International Journal of Entrepreneurship and Innovation*, Vol. 16, No. 4, pp. 291–307.

Drishtee (2021) 'Awards & Recognition,' Available at

https://drishtee.in/about-us/awards-recognition/, Accessed February 14th 2021.

Ianchovichina, E. and Lundstrom, S. (2009) *Inclusive Growth Analytics: Framework and Application*, Washington: The World Bank.

Kaplan, R. S., Serafeim, G. and Tugendhat, E. (2018) 'Inclusive Growth: Profitable Strategies for Tackling Poverty and Inequality,' *Harvard Business Review*, Vol. 96, No. 1, pp. 127-133. (倉田幸信訳「企業の枠を超えたパートナーシップを構築するインクルーシブ・グロース実現への道」『ダイヤモンド・ハーバード・ビジネスレビュー』第43巻第9号，pp. 88-100，ダイヤモンド社，2018年)

――, Serafeim, G. and Tugendhat, E. (2019) *Intelligent Design of Inclusive Growth Strategies*, Boston: Harvard Business School.

Lather, A. S., Garg, S. and Vikas, S. (2009) 'Entrepreneurship as a Strategic Development Intervention to Accelerate Rural Development: The Case of Drishtee,' *Asia Pacific Business Review*, Vol. 5, No. 1, pp. 126-137.

Prahalad, C. K. (2009) *The fortune at the Bottom of the Pyramid: Eradicating Poverty Through Profits, Revised and Updated 5th Anniversary Edition*, Pearson Prentice Hall. (スカイライトコンサルティング訳『ネクスト・マーケット［増補改訂版］』英治出版，2010年)

Suryanarayana, M. H. (2008) '*What Is Exclusive About 'Inclusive Growth'?,' Economic and Political Weekly*, Vol. 43, No. 43, pp. 93-101.

The International Development Research Centre (2011) '*Innovation for Inclusive Development Program Prospectus for 2011-2016 Public version,'* Available at https://www.slideshare.net/uniid-sea/october-2011-innovation-for-inclusive-development-program-prospectus-for-20112016, Accessed February 14th 2021.

Varottil, U. (2018) 'Analysing the CSR Spending Requirements Under Indian Company Law,' in du Plessis, J. J., Varottil, U. and Veldmanin, J. (Ed.), *Globalisation of Corporate Social Responsibility and its Impact on Corporate Governance*, pp. 231-253, Switzerland: Springer International Publishing.

外務省（2020）「インド基礎データ12為替レート1ルピー=1.41円（2020年12月14日）」。Available at https://www.mofa.go.jp/mofaj/area/india/data.html, Accessed February 14th 2021.

加藤徹生著・井上英之監修（2011）『辺境から世界を変える－ソーシャルビジネスが生み出す「村の起業家」』ダイヤモンド社。

佐野孝治他（2012）「インドにおけるソーシャル・ビジネスの展開―海外フィールドワーク実習報告―」『福島大学地域創造』第23巻第2号，pp. 7071-7094。

日本経済新聞（2013）「リコー，人材育成でインドの農村に社員派遣」。Available at https://www.nikkei.com/article/DGXNASFK11032_R11C13A1000000, Accessed February 14th 2021.

渡辺珠子（2012）「インド市場 Drishtee Foundation から農村ビジネスの要諦を学ぶ」。Available at https://diamond.jp/articles/-/16008, Accessed February 14th 2021.

62　企業と社会フォーラム学会誌，第 10 号，pp. 62-79，2021

学界展望

JFBS の 10 年を振り返る：その課題と展望

谷本　寛治

早稲田大学商学学術院商学部教授

　2011 年にスタートした学会「企業と社会フォーラム」（Japan Forum of Business and Society：JFBS）は，今年 10 周年を迎えました。ここでは，JFBS のこの 10 年の足跡を振り返り，改めて JFBS の意義と今後の課題について考えておこうと思います。

　JFBS は，その発足の 2 年前（2009 年 3 月）から活動していた研究会（Forum of Business and Society：FBS，座長谷本）を前身としています。学界，企業，行政，NGO などから 28 人のメンバーが 2 年間で 10 回の研究会を行い，持続可能な社会が求められる時代における企業の経済的・環境的・社会的な役割・責任について，セクターを超えて，理論的・実務的に議論しました（詳しくは, https://j-fbs.jp/events_past%20events.html#p1 参照）。国内外のスピーカーが 30 分報告したあと 1 時間半議論する，この議論中心のスタイルは，今も続いています。2010 年 11 月 APABIS（Asia Pacific Academy of Business in Society）東京カンファレンス（国連大学にて）の開催に協力し，研究会メンバーが 3 人登壇しました。これらの経験を踏まえ，限られたメンバー内での議論にとどめるのではなく，研究会 FBS をオープンな学会に発展させようということになりました。（それ以降の動きは，学会ニュースに出ています。https://j-fbs.jp/news.html）

　当時 2000 年代半ばごろは，CSR ブームが日本でも急速に広がり始めていた時期でした。2008 年の金融危機による景気後退を経てもこの議論は低調になることはなく，2010 年代に入ると，持続可能な発展を求めるグローバルな動き，地球温暖化問題への議論の高まり，CSR 経営にかかわるさまざまな国際規格・標準の広がりなど，時代が大きく変化していました。日本にもその波が押し寄せていました。研究面では国際的には 1990 年代後半から 2000 年代にかけて，この領域への関心が高まり，研究論文も増加し，新しい専門の Journal や学会がスタートしたり，伝統的な学会でも統一テーマに設定されたりしました（このあたりの動向については，谷本「『企業と社会』研究の広がりと課題」『企業と社会フォーラム学会誌』6 号，2017 年参照）。日本ではアカデミックに研究に取り組む研究者は少なかったのですが，関心をもつ人も増えはじめ，専門的な議論を行う場が求められていたと言えます。

　（学会の設立に当たっては，設立趣旨文の作成，会則の設定，個人会員・法人会員への呼びかけ，国内外協力団体への依頼，ロゴ作成依頼，メディア戦略，ウエブサイトの立ち上げ，学会誌作成に

日刊工業新聞の記事

2011 年設立総会の模様

ついて出版社との交渉，設立総会の企画などの準備が行われました。）

JFBS 設立総会は，2011 年 5 月 20 日，三菱地所の協力を得て東京丸の内の丸ビルで開催されました。発足に際し，日刊工業新聞が 5 月 18 日付 1 面に「持続可能な社会発展へ　企業の役割研究─産・学・官・労が結集」と題した記事で紹介をしてくださいました。当初約 140 人の個人会員と，12 社の法人会員の支援を受けてスタートしました（三井物産，ユニリーバ・ジャパン・ホールディングス，積水ハウス，EY 新日本監査法人，損害保険ジャパン，大成建設，東洋経済新報社，日本電気，アクサ生命保険，ソニー，ビューローベリタスジャパン，大和証券。その後，味の素が加わったり法人会員の変動はありましたが，アルビオン，SG ホールディングス，YKK AP，JSR が加わった現在の法人会員は JFBS のサイトを参照下さい。https://j-fbs.jp/members.html）。また凸版印刷には協力組織として，設立当初から参加，協力を得ており，JFBS のロゴは，同社のプロボノの一環として作成していただきました。

設立大会においては次のような視点が提起されました。

1990 年代以降，持続可能な発展（経済・環境・社会）を求めるグローバルな潮流の中，企業の役割・責任が問い直され，CSR が議論されている。企業観の変化や，E・S・G を考慮・評価する市場の変化を踏まえ，持続可能な社会経済システム，企業を構築していくために，関係するステイクホルダー（企業・政府・労組・消費者団体・NGO 等）がその役割を再考し，協働を深める議論が必要である。国内でも 2000 年代以降，CSR がブームとともに議論されその制度化が急速に進展したものの，理解と誤解が混在している。しかし金融危機以降も，CSR への基本的姿勢は変わっておらず，持続可能なシステムを構築する取り組みは少しずつ進んでいる。また東日本大震災の際にも，企業の役割が改めて問われました。社会の中に存在する企業に，責任ある行動，持続可能なビジネスモデルの構築が求められている。

こういった議論を受け，JFBS の設立趣旨は次のように設定されました。

「持続可能な社会経済システムの発展が求められる現在，企業の経済的・社会的・環境的な役割・責任がトータルに問われる時

代になってきています。企業と社会の関係性を問う動きは，先進国から新興国・途上国まで急速な展開を示しており，国際社会との相互依存関係を深化させつつある日本の企業社会にとっても，重要なテーマとなっています。JFBS は，企業と社会の関係をめぐる諸問題について，国内外の学界，産業界，行政，労働界，消費者団体，NPO/NGO などとの幅広い連携を形成し，グローバルな動向を注視しながら，理論と現場と政策をつなぐ場をつくり，学際的に議論・研究することを目的としています。併せて，若手研究者や実務担当者の人材育成にも注力します。」

それから 10 年，企業と社会にかかわる領域，とくにマネジメント，会計，金融の領域において，新たなイニシアチブ，新しい基準が次々に現れ，日本企業は変化への対応に追われています。とくに北米，EU，アジア・パシフィックをはじめ，グローバルにさまざまな議論が展開しており，産業レベル，事業レベルにおいて新しい国際基準や規格が出ています。例えば，サプライチェーンにおけるマネジメント基準の設定，環境・社会に関する非財務情報の開示基準の設定や義務化の動き，金融機関・評価機関による ESG 重視の動きなど，さまざまな動きが企業に対応を迫っています。経済・環境・社会に関するパフォーマンスを考えるトリプルボトムライン（TBL）がシステムに取り組まれる動きが広がっているとも言えます。根底には，企業は誰のために，何のために存在するのか，資本主義市場のあり方まで，国際的に幅広く議論されています。しかしながら，90 年代後半にこの TBL の発想の重要さを唱えた John Elkington 自身は，四半世紀がたった現在，TBL は成功していないと述べています

（2018 International Conference on Sustainability and Responsibility, Germany）。TBL は単なる会計的な指標などではなく，人々の幸福，地球の健康を生み出していくための考え方であり，新しい資本主義システムに経済・環境・社会の 3 つの遺伝子が組み込まれていく必要がある，と主張しています。そのためには，伝統的な市場経済の枠内での議論にとどまるのではなく，企業と NPO/NGO，政府，消費者，さらに大学（研究者 / 学生）など関係するステイクホルダーとの関係，それぞれの行動変容も同時に議論していくことが求められます。JFBS では，当初から企業とステイクホルダー・社会との相互関係を見据える視点で，マネジメント，企業社会，市場システムについて議論してきました。

JFBS の取り組み方としては，以下の点について注視してきました。

- ・持続可能な企業社会について研究する
- ・グローバル社会における日本という視点をもつ
- ・セクター間の連携を深める
- ・研究者と実務家が議論し交流する場（オープンなプラットフォーム）をつくる
- ・責任あるリーダーを育成する
- ・社会変革への触媒となる

こういった視点から JFBS は，設立当初から海外の関係学会や大学と積極的に連携しています。とくに APBIS（現在は ABIS に統合），EABIS（European Academy of Business in Society：現在は ABIS に名称変更，ベルギー），International Conference on Sustainability and Responsibility（2 年に一度開催，ドイツ），CSR Asia（香港），BSR（Business for Social Responsibility，アメリカ），さらに大学研究機関としては，Free

University Berlin（ドイツ）の East Asian Studies, Cologne Business School（ドイツ）の Center for Advanced Sustainable Management, National Taipei University（台湾）の Center for CSR, Murdoch University（オーストラリア）の Centre for Responsible Citizenship and Sustainability, Inha University（韓国）の Sustainability Management Research Institute, Russian Business Ethics Network（ロシア）などと連携をしています。

　国内においては，グローバル・コンパクト・ネットワーク・ジャパン，企業市民協議会（CBCC），経済人コー円卓会議日本委員会，日本コーポレート・ガバナンス・ネットワークなどと連携しています。こういった団体や法人会員からは，これまで年次大会や研究会においてもたくさんのスピーカーに登壇いただいています。

　学会が取り扱う主な研究テーマとしては，以下のものが挙げられます（*は当初の項目に追記したもの）。

・企業と社会の関係，持続可能な発展，SDGs*，サーキュラーエコノミー*，公共政策
・CSR 経営，コーポレート・ガバナンス，経営倫理
・環境経営，環境会計，環境保全
・消費者，安全・衛生，労働・人権，サプライチェーン
・社会貢献，ソーシャル・マーケティング，CRM，ソーシャル・プロダクト
・ステイクホルダー・エンゲージメント，情報開示／報告書，CSR 教育
・企業価値，レピュテーション，SRI，ESG 投資*

・NPO/NGO，セクター間の協働／提携，国際支援
・マルチ・ステイクホルダー・プロセス，グローバル・ガバナンス，国際基準
・ソーシャル・ビジネス，ソーシャル・イノベーション
・国際比較，教育方法*など

　もちろんこれですべての課題を網羅しているわけではありませんが，「企業と社会」というテーマは幅広く，関連する領域は非常に広いと言えます。したがって，研究としては関連諸領域との連携も必要ですし，アプローチとしては学際的な視点も求められます。企業経営の現場からすると，CSR やサステナビリティにかかわる課題は，関連の部署との連携の中で取り組まなければならない課題です。

　JFBS がこれまで行ってきた基本活動は次の通りです。

・9 月に開催する年次大会（ドクトラル・ワークショップも開催）
・年 3〜4 回開催する定期研究会
・研究助成金の提供
・学会誌（年報）の発行（千倉書房刊）
・海外提携学会・組織との協働
・ウエブサイトによる情報発信，国際会議や海外 Journal に関する情報提供など

　JFBS は，当初から国内外のネットワークを通じて研究者や実務家が集まる場であり，多様なスピーカーが集まってきました。ここでは，第 1 回から第 10 回までの年次大会のテーマとキーノート・スピーカーを振り返っておきます。なお各回の企画セッションのテーマと報告者は，後段**資料 1** にまとめています。

年次大会テーマ一覧

2011 – 2021　JFBS 年次大会テーマ		
2011	第 1 回	持続可能な発展とマルチ・ステイクホルダー：Sustainable Development and Multi-Stakeholders Keynote Speakers: ■ Juliet Roper (Professor, Waikato Management School, The University of Waikato, New Zealand) ■ Jeremy Prepscius (Vice President, BSR Asia, Hong Kong)
2012	第 2 回	持続可能な発展とイノベーション：Sustainable Development and Innovation Keynote Speaker: ■ Daniele Chauvel (Research Professor, SKEMA Business School, France)
2013	第 3 回	CSR とコーポレート・ガバナンス：CSR and Corporate Governance Keynote Speaker：■ Joachim Schwalbach (Professor, School of Business and Economics, Humboldt University of Berlin, Germany)
2014	第 4 回	持続可能性と戦略：Sustainability and Strategy Keynote Speakers: ■ CB Bhattacharya (Professor, European School of Management and Technology, Germany) ■ Isamu Wada (CEO, Sekisui House)
2015	第 5 回	企業家精神とサステナブル・イノベーション：Entrepreneurship and Sustainable Innovation Keynote Speakers: ■ Richard Welford (Chairman, CSR Asia, Hong Kong) ■ Yoshimitsu Kobayashi (Chairman, Member of the Board, Mitsubishi Chemical Holdings Corporation)
2016	第 6 回	社会的課題とマーケティング：Marketing and Social Change Keynote Speakers: ■ Dirk Matten (Professor, Schulich School of Business, York University, Canada) ■ Fulvio Guarneri (President and CEO, Unilever Japan Customer Marketing)
2017	第 7 回	サステナブル・エンタープライズ—企業の持続性と社会性：Sustainable Enterprise: Revisiting an Enterprise Concept Keynote Speakers: ■ Jeremy Moon (Professor, Department of Inter-cultural Communication and Management, Copenhagen Business School, Denmark) ■ Masaru Terada (President, Terada Honke)
2018	第 8 回	企業と社会の戦略的コミュニケーション：Strategic Communications in Business and Society Keynote Speakers: ■ Carol Adams (Professor, Durham Business School, Durham University, UK) ■ Shuri Fukunaga (Chief Executive Officer, Burson-Marsteller)
2019	第 9 回	サステナビリティ人材の育成と経営教育：CSR/Sustainability in Management Education Keynote Speakers: ■ Elisabeth Fröhlich (President, Cologne Business School, Germany) ■ Toshio Arima (Chairman of the Board, Global Compact Network Japan)
2021	第 10 回	サーキュラーエコノミーを目指して：Circular Economy Transition: Exploring the Institutional, Organizational & Behavioral Dimensions Keynote Speakers: ■ R. Edward Freeman (Professor, Darden School of Business, University of Virginia, USA) ■ Valentina Carbone (Professor, ESCP, Paris, France) ■ Marjut Hannonen (Minister-Counsellor, Head, Delegation of the European Union to Japan) ■ Tomomi Fukumoto (Executive Officer, Division COO, Corporate Sustainability Division, Suntory Holdings)

*2020 年は Covid-19 の影響で中止・延期になりました。所属・肩書は当時のものです。

2017 年第 7 回大会より

左：Schwalbach 教授　右：Moon 教授

2018 年第 8 回大会より

Adams 教授キーノート・スピーチ

ところで，2013 年の第 3 回大会は，ドイツフンボルト大学の Joachim Schwalbach 教授が主導してきた International Conference on Corporate Sustainability and Responsibility と共同開催を行いました（第 5 回，第 7 回も）。第 3 回大会時は，Japanese-German Center Berlin (JDZB) とも共催し，資金援助を受けることができました。

また，2016 年の第 6 回大会では日本マーケティング学会と，2018 年の第 8 回大会では日本広報学会とも連携し，協力を得て開催することができました。

これまで海外の Journal との連携も行ってきました。第 3 回大会において Journal of Corporate Citizenship（Greenleaf Publishing）と連携し，谷本が Guest Editor となり，Special Issue "Japanese Approaches to CSR" が組まれました。特集号は 2014 年の Issue 56 として発行されました。第 5 回大会では，Corporate Governance: the international journal of business in society（Emerald）と連携し，特集号 Special Issue "Entrepreneurship and Sustainable Innovation" が同様に組まれました。ただ最終的にアクセプトされた論文が少なかったためそれらは通常号に回され，特別号は発刊されませんでした。

JFBSの主な特徴を改めてまとめておきます。

- ・オープンなネットワークの構築をめざし，国（地域），セクターを超えた連携に務めていること。会員の多様性があり（個人会員：大学人 50 ％，企業人 35 ％，NGO 他 15 ％。法人会員の参画），国内外の連携組織との交流がなされています。
- ・テーマに沿ったスピーカーを広く招待していること。とくにキーノート・スピーカーは，海外から当該領域で著名な研究者と，日本のトップ経営者が登壇しています。企画セッションにおいても，各テーマの専門家（研究者・実務家）を招待し，突っ込んだ議論をしています。
- ・オープンな Call For Paper を行っていること。年次大会における CFP は，会員のみならず国内外へオープンに報告を募っており（毎年 10 か国前後から参加者が集まり），英語と日本語のセッションが組まれています。
- ・オープンな交流の場を作っていること。とくに年次大会においては，ランチ，コーヒーブレイク，ウェルカムパーティ，フェアウェルドリンクなどオープンな場を提供し，参加者間の交流を図っています。

2019 年第 9 回大会より

Fröhlich 教授キーノート・スピーチ

B Corp Asia のセッション

・ドクトラルワークショップを国内外の学生を交えて行ってきたこと。さらに優秀な報告に対しては助成金（最大 10 万円）を提供してきました。

・研究助成金を毎年提供してきたこと（1 件 20 万円）。「企業と社会」関連領域の研究促進を図ってきました。

・オープンな年報「企業と社会フォーラム学会誌」の発行（日本語・英語の論文）。一般投稿論文は，会員にとどまらず，国内外オープンに公募し，ダブル・ブラインド・レビューを行っています。
【補足】これまで学術論文の投稿は（第 2 号〜第 10 号）43 本で採択されたのは 18 本，採択率は 41.8％でした。事例紹介・解説の投稿は（第 5 号〜第 10 号）9 本で採択されたのは 5 本，採択率は 55.5％でした。レビュアーとして協力していただいた方々のお名前は，後段**資料 2**をご覧下さい。

以上のようなユニークな面は伸ばしつつ，今後の 10 年を見据えた課題・展望として次のような点を挙げておきたいと思います。

・会員の拡大。関連領域で研究している研究者，とくに若手研究者を巻き込んでい

くことが求められます。法人会員についてももう少し参加企業を広げていくことが期待されます。

・研究助成活動の再開。現在予算の制約で一時停止しているため，早い再開が期待されます。

・実務的なセミナーの開催。研究者と実務家の交流を図ってきていますが，さらに実務的なセミナーやエグゼクティブを巻き込んだセミナーなどの開催や，広く一般向けのセミナーやイベントなどの取り組みも，今後検討する必要があるかもしれません。

・連携組織との協働の活発化。連携している国内外の組織と，これまで以上に活発な研究活動・協働が求められるでしょう。

・ウェビナーの活用。コロナ禍において，2020 年 12 月，2021 年 1 月，5 月に海外のスピーカーとともにオンライン研究会やシンポジウムを開催しました。ポストコロナにおいてはこのスタイルも積極的に活用し，学会活動の幅を広げていくことが期待できると思います。

資料 1

　各大会のキーノート・スピーカー，企画セッションとそのスピーカーを，資料としてまとめておきます（なお所属・肩書は当時のものです。また日本語表記のセッションでの使用言語は日本語，英語表記は英語です）。

■ 2011 年　第 1 回年次大会（9/16）

「持続可能な発展とマルチ・ステイクホルダー」

　"Sustainable Development and Multi-Stakeholders"

Keynote Speakers

・Juliet Roper (Professor, Waikato Management School, The University of Waikato, New Zealand)

・Jeremy Prepscius (Vice President, BSR Asia, Hong Kong)

Plenary Session：日本における円卓会議の可能性

・関正雄（損害保険ジャパン CSR 統括部長）

・佐藤正弘（元・内閣府／京都大学経済研究所准教授）

・田村太郎（ダイバーシティ研究所代表理事）

・加来栄一（日本労働組合総連合会）

・阿南久（全国消費者団体連絡会事務局長）

・谷本寛治（一橋大学大学院商学研究科教授）

司会：水口剛（高崎経済大学経済学部教授）

■ 2012 年　第 2 回年次大会（9/20-21）

「持続可能な発展とイノベーション」"Sustainable Development and Innovation"

Keynote Speaker

・Daniele Chauvel (Research Professor, SKEMA Business School, France)

Plenary Session 1：Innovation for Sustainable Development

・Daniele Chauvel (Research Professor, SKEMA Business School, France)

・Ray Bremner (President & CEO, Unilever Japan Customer Marketing)

・Botaro Hirosaki (Special Advisor, NEC)

・Kanji Tanimoto (Professor, School of Commerce, Waseda University)

Chair：Masahiro Okada (Associate Professor, Graduate School of Business and Commerce, Keio University)

Plenary Session 2：消費を通じた社会的課題解決

・大平修司（千葉商科大学商経学部准教授）

・園部靖史（高千穂大学商学部准教授）

・Sumire Stanislawski（早稲田大学商学部助手）

Chair：Florian Kohlbacher (Head of Business & Economics Section, German Institute for Japanese Studies)

Plenary Session 3：日本の企業社会とイノベーション

- ・嶋村和行（大成建設環境本部副本部長）
- ・西山圭太（経済産業省経済産業政策局大臣官房審議官経済社会政策担当）
- ・仁平章（日本労働組合総連合会経済政策局長）
- ・鈴木亨（特定非営利活動法人北海道グリーンファンド理事長）
- ・古谷由紀子（公益社団法人日本消費生活アドバイザー・コンサルタント協会常任顧問）

司会：金井一頼（大阪商業大学総合経営学部教授）

■ 2013 年　第 3 回年次大会（9/19-20）

International Conference on Corporate Sustainability and Responsibility ／ Japanese-German Center Berlin（JDZB）との共催

「CSR とコーポレート・ガバナンス」 "CSR and Corporate Governance"

Keynote Speaker

- ・Joachim Schwalbach (Professor, School of Business and Economics, Humboldt University of Berlin, Germany)

Plenary Session 1：CSR and Corporate Governance: Comparative Study of European Companies and Japanese

- ・Verena Blechinger-Talcott (Professor, Japanese Politics and Political Economy, Free University of Berlin, Germany)
- ・Masayuki Kinoshita (Representative Director, Senior Executive Managing Officer, MITSUI & CO., LTD.)
- ・Takahiro Ogasawara (Chief Corporate Responsibility Officer, AXA Life Insurance)
- ・Carsten Schmitz-Hoffmann (Director, Business Unit Private Sector Cooperation, Deutsche Gesellschaft für Internationale Zusammenarbeit (GIZ) GmbH, Germany)
- ・Kanji Tanimoto (Professor, School of Commerce, Waseda University)

Chair：Gregory Jackson (Professor, School of Business and Economics, Free University of Berlin, Germany)

Organized 1：日本企業のコーポレート・ガバナンス "Corporate Governance of Japanese Companies"

- ・Gregory Jackson (Professor, School of Business and Economics, Free University of Berlin, Germany)
- ・宮島英昭（早稲田大学商学部教授）
- ・中山泰男（セコム常務取締役）
- ・立石文雄（オムロン取締役会長）

司会：荻野博司（朝日新聞社企画委員／NPO 法人日本コーポレート・ガバナンス・ネットワーク企画委員長）

Organized 2：Compliance and Strategic Choice

- ・Akitsugu Era (Vice President, BlackRock Japan)

・Herbert Hemming (President and Representative Director, Bosch Japan)

・Kiyomi Saito (President, JBond Totan Securities)

・Fumitoshi Sato (Managing Director, Horiba)

・Masao Seki (Managing Director, Sompo Japan Environmental Foundation / Senior Advisor CSR, Sompo Japan / Associate Professor, Meiji University Management School)

Chair：Kyoko Sakuma-Keck (Senior Researcher, Solvay Business School of Economics and Management, Belgium)

Organized 3：Supply Chain Management

・Alan Aicken (Vice President and Chief Sustainability Officer, Huawei Technologies, China)

・Nick Barter (Senior Lecturer, Asia-Pacific Centre for Sustainable Enterprise, Griffith University, Australia)

・Yoshitaka Okada (Professor, Faculty of Liberal Arts, Sophia University)

・Hitoshi Suzuki (President, Institute for International Socio-Economic Studies)

Chair：Katsuhiko Kokubu (Professor, Graduate School of Business Administration, Kobe University)

Organized 4：ビジネスと人権 "Business and Human Rights"

・熊谷謙一（公益財団法人国際労働財団副事務長）

・黒田かをり（一般財団法人 CSO ネットワーク事務局長・理事）

・Luigi Colantuoni (President, Tokyo Branch, Total Trading Int'l, S.A.)

・大久保和孝（新日本有限責任監査法人シニアパートナー）

司会：石田寛（NPO 法人経済人コー円卓会議日本委員会事務局長）

Plenary Session 2：CSR and Corporate Governance: Integrated Report

・Carol Adams (Director, Integrated Horizons / Professor, Monash Sustainability Institute, Monash University, Australia)

・Alan Aicken (Vice President and Chief Sustainability Officer, Huawei Technologies, China)

・Jiang Wanjun (Associate Professor, Guanghua School of Management, Peking University, China)

・Hidemi Tomita (Lloyd's Register Quality Assurance Limited / Chair, GRI Multi-stakeholder Committee)

Chair：Joachim Schwalbach (Professor, School of Business and Economics, Humboldt University of Berlin, Germany)

■ 2014 年　第 4 回年次大会 (9/18-19)

「持続可能性と戦略」 "Sustainability and Strategy"

Keynote Speakers

・CB Bhattacharya (Professor, European School of Management and Technology, Germany)

・和田勇（積水ハウス代表取締役会長兼 CEO）

Plenary Session 1：Sustainability and Strategy　「持続可能性と戦略」

・Nick Barter (Associate Professor, Asia-Pacific Centre for Sustainable Enterprise, Griffith University,

Australia)

・CB Bhattacharya (Professor, European School of Management and Technology, Germany)

・和田勇（積水ハウス代表取締役会長兼 CEO）

Chair and Panelist：Masahiro Okada (Professor, Graduate School of Business Administration, Keio University)

Organized 1：Sustainability and Brand Management

・David Hessekiel (Founder and President, Cause Marketing Forum, USA)

・Hidenori Imazu (Manager, Toppan Idea Center, Toppan Printing)

・Takeshi Ohta (Deputy Director, Planning Section, CSV Management Dept., CSV Division, Kirin Holdings)

Chair and Panelist：Tobias Bielenstein (Managing Partner, Branding- Institute, Germany)

Organized 2：Sustainable Strategy and Emerging Markets

・Ashir Ahmed (Associate Professor, Institute for Advanced Study, Kyushu University)

・Yoko Nagashima (Japan Environmental Manager, Hewlett-Packard Japan)

・Ashok Roy (Managing Partner, jED)

Chair：Masahiro Okada (Professor, Graduate School of Business Administration, Keio University)

Organized 3：持続可能性と金融市場

・金井司（三井住友信託銀行経営企画部理事・CSR 担当部長）

・黒崎美穂（ブルームバーグ ESG スペシャリスト）

・山本利明（大阪電気通信大学金融経済学部教授）

・横山正浩（大和証券グループ本社広報部担当部長）

司会：雨宮寛（コーポレートシチズンシップ代表）

Organized 4：Green Management

・Takenobu Shiina (General Manager, Environmental Sustainability Strategy Department, Corporate Communication Division, Suntory Holdings)

・Maho Takahashi (Manager, Charity & Campaign, Lush Japan)

・Keiko Zaima (Professor, Faculty of Business Administration, Kyoto Sangyo University)

Chair：Gabriel Eweje (Associate Professor, College of Business, Massey University, New Zealand)

Plenary Session 2 (Wrap-up)：Sustainability and Strategy

・Nick Barter (Associate Professor, Asia-Pacific Centre for Sustainable Enterprise, Griffith University, Australia)

・Tobias Bielenstein (Managing Partner, Branding- Institute, Germany)

・Hiroshi Amemiya (President, Corporate Citizenship)

・Gabriel Eweje (Associate Professor, College of Business, Massey University, New Zealand)

Chair：Masahiro Okada (Professor, Graduate School of Business Administration, Keio University)

■ 2015 年　第 5 回年次大会（9/10-11）

International Conference on Corporate Sustainability and Responsibility ／ CSR Asia との共催

「企業家精神とサステナブル・イノベーション」
"Entrepreneurship and Sustainable Innovation"

Keynote Speakers

・Richard Welford (Chairman, CSR Asia, Hong Kong)

・Yoshimitsu Kobayashi (Chairman, Member of the Board, Mitsubishi Chemical Holdings Corporation ／ Chairman, Japan Association of Corporate Executives)

Plenary Session 1：Intrapreneurship and Sustainable Innovation

・Alan Aicken (Vice President and Chief Sustainability Officer, Huawei Technologies, China)

・Yukiko Araki (Corporate Officer, Executive General Manager, CSR and Environmental Strategy Division, Hitachi)

・Luigi Colantuoni (Chief Representative for Japan, Total ／ President, Total Trading International, Tokyo Branch)

・Joachim Schwalbach (Professor, School of Business and Economics, Humboldt-University of Berlin, Germany)

・Kanji Tanimoto (Professor, School of Commerce, Waseda University)

Chair：Sadao Nagaoka (Professor, Faculty of Economics, Tokyo Keizai University)

Organized 1：社会的責任のある事業と法人形態

・岸本幸子（パブリックリソースセンター事務局長）

・篠健司（パタゴニア日本支社環境プログラム・ディレクター）

・竹内英二（日本政策金融公庫総合研究所主席研究員）

司会：土肥将敦（法政大学現代福祉学部教授）

Organized 2：Fail Forward

・Ashley Good (Founder and CEO, Fail Forward, Canada)

・Zaw Naing (Managing Director, Mandalay Technology, Myanmar)

・Yukie Ohno (Merchandising Dept., Daichi Wo Mamoru Kai)

Chair：Hiroshi Amemiya (CEO, Corporate Citizenship Japan)

Organized 3：Business and Human Rights

・Richard Welford (Chairman, CSR Asia, Hong Kong)

・Daisuke Takahashi (Partner, Shinwa Sohgoh Law Offices)

・Saul Takahashi (Regional Representative for Japan, Business and Human Rights Resource Centre)

・Keiichi Ushijima (Japan Area CCaSS Leader, Managing Director, Ernst and Young Shinnihon LLC)

Chair：Yasunobu Sato (Professor, Research Center for Sustainable Peace, the Institute for Advanced Global Studies, The University of Tokyo)

Organized 4：Sustainable Regional Innovation

・Kazushi Kaneto (President, The Islands' Company)

・Eisuke Tachikawa (Founder / Design Strategist, NOSIGNER)

・Sayaka Watanabe (CEO and Founder, re:terra)

Chair：Nobuyoshi Ohmuro (Professor, Faculty of Business Administration, Kyoto Sangyo University)

Plenary Session 2 (Wrap-up)：Entrepreneurship and Sustainable Innovation

・Alan Aicken (Vice President and Chief Sustainability Officer, Huawei Technologies, China)

・Hiroshi Amemiya (CEO, Corporate Citizenship Japan)

・Masaatsu Doi (Associate Professor, Faculty of Social Policy and Administration, Hosei University)

・Nobuyosi Ohmuro (Professor, Faculty of Business Administration, Kyoto Sangyo University)

Chair：Robert Hales (Senior Lecturer, Department of Business Strategy and Innovation, Griffith University, Australia)

■ 2016 年　第 6 回年次大会（9/8-9）日本マーケティング学会の後援

「社会的課題とマーケティング」"Marketing and Social Change"

Keynote Speakers

・Dirk Matten (Professor, Schulich School of Business, York University, Canada)

・Fulvio Guarneri (President and CEO, Unilever Japan Customer Marketing)

Plenary Session 1：Marketing and Social Change

・Gabriel Eweje (Associate Professor, Massey Business School, Massey University, New Zealand)

・Kyoko Fukukawa (Senior Lecturer, School of Management, University of Bradford, UK)

・Fulvio Guarneri (President and CEO, Unilever Japan Customer Marketing)

・Dirk Matten (Professor, Schulich School of Business, York University, Canada)

Chair：Gabriel Eweje (Associate Professor, Massey Business School, Massey University, New Zealand)

Organized 1：都市開発とイノベーティブ・マーケティング

・古川一郎（一橋大学大学院商学研究科教授）

・広瀬雄樹（積水ハウス CSR 室長）

・小山健（積和グランドマスト代表取締役社長）

・村上孝憲（三菱地所開発推進部新機能開発室副長）

・松田智生（三菱総合研究所プラチナ社会研究センター主席研究員・チーフプロデューサー）

司会：畢滔滔（立正大学経営学部教授）

Organized 2：持続可能性とイノベーティブ・マーケティング

・畑中晴雄（花王経営サポート部門サステナビリティ推進グループ部長）

・西尾チヅル（筑波大学大学院ビジネス科学研究科）

・小竹茜氏（LIXIL パブリックアフェアーズ部門グローバルコーポレートリスポンシビリティ推進室室長）

・田代裕貴（王子ネピアマーケティング本部長）

司会：大平修司（千葉商科大学商経学部准教授）

Organized 3：社会的課題とイノベーティブ・マーケティング

・有本幸泰（イオントップバリュマーケティング本部ブランドマネジメント部）

・小寺徹（JTB コーポレートセールス／ CSV 開発機構専務理事）

・野田美奈子（SG ホールディングス総務部広報・CSR ユニットマネジャー）

・大瀬良伸（東洋大学経営学部准教授）

司会：永井朝子（BSR 日本ディレクター）

Organized 4：日本マーケティング学会セッション

・水越康介（首都大学東京大学院社会科学研究科准教授）

・横田浩一（横田アソシエイツ代表）

司会：大平修司（千葉商科大学商経学部准教授）

Organized 5：地方創生とイノベーティブ・マーケティング

・半谷栄寿（あすびと福島代表理事）

・水越康介（首都大学東京大学院社会科学研究科准教授）

・須賀大介（福岡移住計画主催）

・和田智行（小高ワーカーズベース代表）

司会：今津秀紀（凸版印刷トッパンアイデアセンターマーケティング企画部長）

Plenary Session 2 (Wrap-up)：社会的課題とマーケティング

・今津秀紀（凸版印刷トッパンアイデアセンターマーケティング企画部長）

・永井朝子（BSR 日本ディレクター）

・西尾チヅル（筑波大学大学院ビジネス科学研究科）

・大平修司（千葉商科大学商経学部准教授）

司会：福川恭子（Senior Lecturer, School of Management, University of Bradford, UK）

■ **2017 年　第 7 回年次大会（9/7-8）** International Conference on Corporate Sustainability and Responsibility との共催

「サステナブル・エンタープライズ：企業の持続性と社会性」

　"Sustainable Enterprise: Revisiting an Enterprise Concept"

Keynote Speakers

・Jeremy Moon (Professor, Department of Intercultural Communication and Management, Copenhagen Business School, Denmark)

・Masaru Terada (President, Terada Honke)

Plenary Session 1：Sustainable Enterprise: Revisiting an Enterprise Concept

・Sarah Jastram (Professor, Department of Strategy and Leadership, Hamburg School of Business Administration, Germany)

・Katsuhiko Kokubu (Professor, Graduate School of Business Administration, Kobe University)

・Jeremy Moon (Professor, Department of Intercultural Communication and Management, Copenhagen Business School, Denmark)

・Joachim Schwalbach (Professor, School of Business and Economics, Humboldt-University of Berlin,

Germany)

・Masaru Terada (President, Terada Honke)

Chair：René Schmidpeter (Professor, Center for Advanced Sustainable Management, Cologne Business School, Germany)

Organized 1：長寿企業から学ぶ「企業」像

・河崎保徳（ロート製薬東京支社広報・CSV 推進部部長）

・新田見篤（イトーキソリューション開発本部 Eco ソリューション開発室課長）

・原良憲（京都大学経営管理大学院教授）

司会：大室悦賀（京都産業大学経営学部教授）

Organized 2：サステナビリティと地域金融の在り方

・江上広行（電通国際情報サービス金融ソリューション事業部 VCF エバンジェリスト）

・斎藤栄太郎（全国信用協同組合連合会総合企画部副部長）

・三島大尚（全国信用協同組合連合会総合企画部主任調査役）

・和田裕介（日本政策金融公庫国民生活事業融資企画部ソーシャル・ビジネス支援グループグループリーダー）

・藤井良広（環境金融研究機構理事長）

司会：山本利明（大阪電気通信大学金融経済学部教授）

Organized 3：ソーシャル・ビジネスの組織戦略

・鳥居希（バリューブックス取締役）

・米澤旦（明治学院大学社会学部准教授）

・土肥将敦（法政大学現代福祉学部教授）

・大室悦賀（京都産業大学経営学部教授）

司会：金井一頼（大阪商業大学総合経営学部教授）

Organized 4：サステナブル・ビジネスモデルの構築

・惣宇利紀子（公文教育研究会社長室調査企画チームリーダー）

・阿部哲也（IKEUCHI ORGANIC 代表取締役社長）

・土肥将敦（法政大学現代福祉学部教授）

司会：鷲田祐一（一橋大学大学院商学研究科教授）

Plenary Session 2 (Wrap-up)：Sustainable Enterprise: Revisiting an Enterprise Concept

・Kazuyori Kanai (Professor, Faculty of Business Administration, Osaka University of Commerce)

・Nobuyoshi Ohmuro (Professor, Faculty of Business Administration, Kyoto Sangyo University)

・Yuichi Washida (Professor, Graduate School of Commerce and Management, Hitotsubashi University)

・Toshiaki Yamamoto (Professor, Faculty of Financial Economy, Osaka Electro-Communication University)

Chair：René Schmidpeter (Professor, Center for Advanced Sustainable Management, Cologne Business School, Germany)

■ 2018 年　第 8 回年次大会（9/6-7）日本広報学会との共催

「企業と社会の戦略的コミュニケーション」

"Strategic Communications in Business and Society"

Keynote Speakers

・Carol Adams (Professor, Durham Business School, Durham University, UK)

・Shuri Fukunaga (Chief Executive Officer, Burson-Marsteller)

Plenary Session 1：Strategic Communications in Business and Society

・Carol Adams (Professor, Durham Business School, Durham University, UK)

・Shuri Fukunaga (Chief Executive Officer, Burson-Marsteller)

・Masaki Tomioka (Senior General Manager, Corporate Brand Strategy Department, Corporate Sustainability Division, Suntory Holdings)

・Raymond Shelton (Executive Officer, Coca-Cola Bottlers Japan Holdings)

Chair：Daniel McFarlane (Adjunct Lecturer, School of Global Studies, Thammasat University, Thailand)

Organized 1：広報から見た CSR とコミュニケーション ＜日本広報学会共催セッション＞

・上野征洋（社会情報大学院大学学長／日本広報学会副会長）

・北見幸一（東京都市大学都市生活学部／大学院環境情報学研究科准教授）

・佐桑徹（経済広報センター常任理事）

・薗部靖史（東洋大学社会学部准教授）

司会：川北眞紀子（南山大学経営学部教授）

Organized 2：消費者とのコミュニケーション

・笹谷秀光（伊藤園顧問）

・高堰博英（三井物産経営企画部業務室次長）

・間宮孝治（電通新ソーシャル・デザイン・エンジン事務局長）

司会：西尾チヅル（筑波大学大学院ビジネス科学研究科教授）

Organized 3：投資家や投資機関とのコミュニケーション

・井垣勉（オムロン執行役員グローバルインベスター＆ブランドコミュニケーション本部長）

・牛島慶一（EY 新日本有限責任監査法人気候変動・サステナビリティサービス CCaSS リーダープリンシパル）

・鳥光健太郎（KDDI サステナビリティ推進室長）

・松本加代（経済産業省経済産業政策局企業会計室室長）

司会：今津秀紀（凸版印刷トッパンアイデアセンターコーポレートコミュニケーション部部長）

Organized 4：メディア・コミュニケーション

・田中太郎（日経 BP 日経 ESG 編集長）

・宮崎伸夫（朝日新聞社総合プロデュース室室長）

・高広伯彦（社会情報大学院大学客員教授）

司会：荻野博司（東洋学園大学グローバルコミュニケーション学部教授）

Organized 5：ESG 関連リスク対応の実務

・中野竹司（奥・片山・佐藤法律事務所弁護士／公認会計士）

・鈴木仁史（鈴木総合法律事務所弁護士）

・松原稔（りそな銀行アセットマネジメント部責任投資グループグループリーダー）

司会：齊藤誠（齊藤法律事務所弁護士）

Plenary Session 2 (Wrap-up)：企業と社会の戦略的コミュニケーション

・川北眞紀子（南山大学教授経営学部教授）

・西尾チヅル（筑波大学教授大学院ビジネス科学研究科教授）

・今津秀紀（凸版印刷トッパンアイデアセンターコーポレートコミュニケーション部部長）

・荻野博司（東洋学園大学グローバルコミュニケーション学部教授）

Chair：Daniel McFarlane (Adjunct Lecturer, School of Global Studies, Thammasat University, Thailand)

■ 2019 年　第 9 回年次大会（9/5-6）B Corp Asia の協力

「サステナビリティ人材の育成と経営教育」

"CSR/Sustainability in Management Education"

Keynote Speakers

・Elisabeth Fröhlich (President, Cologne Business School, Germany)

・Toshio Arima (Chairman of the Board, Global Compact Network Japan)

Plenary Session 1：CSR/Sustainability in Management Education

・Toshio Arima (Chairman of the Board, Global Compact Network Japan)

・Elisabeth Fröhlich (President, Cologne Business School, Germany)

・Takayuki Kitajima (Representative Director, General Counsel, Unilever Japan Holdings)

・Michele John (Professor, Faculty of Science and Technology, Curtin University, Australia)

Chair：Kyoko Fukukawa (Professor, Faculty of Commerce and Management, Hitotsubashi University)

Organized 1：企業における「ビジネスと人権」教育・研修の課題

・菊池浩（法務省人権擁護局局長）

・齊藤誠（ビジネスと人権ロイヤーズネットワーク）

・杉本茂（ANA ホールディングス CSR 推進部）

司会：足達英一郎（日本総研創発戦略センター理事）

Organized 2：Sustainability Leadership Training

・Gefei Yin (Chief Expert, GoldenBee Corporate Social Responsibility Consulting, China)

・Masahiro Okada (Professor, Graduate School of Business and Commerce, Keio University)

・Tomoko Hasegawa (Director, SDGs Promotion Bureau, Keidanren: Japan Business Federation)

Chair：Masao Seki (Senior Advisor on CSR, Sompo Japan Nipponkoa Insurance)

Organized 3：Higher Education for Sustainability

・Akiko Imai (Professor, Faculty of Global Business, Showa Women's University)

・Joel Malen (Associate Professor, School of Commerce, Waseda University)

・Philip Sugai (Professor, Doshisha Business School, Doshisha University)

・Yoshiteru Uramoto (Professor, Center for Global Education, Sophia University)

Chair：Hiroshi Amemiya (Head of Japan, Arabesque S-Ray GmbH Japan branch)

Organized 4：サステナビリティ人材の育成におけるメディアの役割

・木幡美子（フジテレビジョン総務局 CSR 推進室部長）

・倉持裕和（朝日新聞社 CSR 推進部次長）

・堅達京子（NHK エンタープライズ制作本部情報文化番組エグゼクティブ・プロデューサー）

司会：牛島慶一（EY 新日本有限責任監査法人気候変動・サステナビリティサービス CCaSS リーダープリンシパル）

Plenary Session 2 (Wrap-up)：CSR/Sustainability in Management Education

・Masao Seki (Senior Advisor on CSR, Sompo Japan Nipponkoa Insurance)

・Hiroshi Amemiya (Head of Japan, Arabesque S-Ray GmbH Japan branch)

・Keiichi Ushijima (Japan CCaSS Leader, Principal, Climate Change and Sustainability Services, Ernst &Young ShinNihon)

Chair：Kyoko Fukukawa (Professor, Faculty of Commerce and Management, Hitotsubashi University)

資料 2

以下は，JFBS 学会誌のレビュアーとして貢献していただいた方々のお名前です。記して感謝いたします（敬称略）。

Haider Mohammad Badrul, Silke Bustamante, Mohammad Badrul Haider, Mohammad Tazul Islam, Jaeho Moon, Emmanuel Mutisya, Gustavo Tanaka, Md. Shahid Ullah, Qi Wu, Edward Yagi 青木慶，稲葉祐之，梅津光弘，大月博司，大平修司，大室悦賀，岡照二，岡田正大，梶原晃，加藤敬太，金井一頼，國部克彦，後藤祐一，阪智香，坂下玄哲，佐々木利廣，佐藤正弘，澤井実，澤田直宏，髙美穂，髙田一樹，竹林正人，谷本寛治，土肥将敦，中尾悠利子，中園宏幸，西尾チヅル，西谷公孝，野林晴彦，藤田誠，堀口真司，八木迪幸，矢鋪秀俊，山田仁一郎，鑓目雅，横山恵子

学会ニュース

1. 部会（2020 年 9 月～2021 年 5 月）報告
2. 第 10 回年次大会（2021 年 9 月 2～3 日）案内

1.　部会報告

第 31 回東日本部会
・日　時　2020 年 9 月 5 日（土）13：30～16：45
　　　　　　　オンライン（Zoom）
・テーマ・報告者等
　(1) 改正消費者契約法と企業経営への影響
　　【報告者】池内博一准教授（追手門学院大学経営学部）
　(2) 日本中小企業におけるグリーンマネジメントに関する調査：経過報告
　　【報告者】福川恭子教授（一橋大学大学院経営管理研究科）
　(3) ポストコロナと「企業と社会」
　　【報告者】谷本寛治教授（早稲田大学商学学術院商学部）
　　【司　会】谷本寛治教授（早稲田大学商学学術院商学部）

第 32 回東日本部会
・日　時　2020 年 12 月 12 日（土）13：30～16：45（JST）
　　　　　　　オンライン（Zoom）
・テーマ・報告者等
　(1) 外生的ショックと CSR 活動
　　【報告者】吉田賢一助手（早稲田大学ビジネス・ファイナンス研究センター）
　(2) 中国の社会的企業とそのエコシステム － 2019 年の発展状況と課題
　　【報告者】金仁仙副教授（対外経済貿易大学政府管理学院，日中韓社会的経済研究中心主任）
　(3) B Corp Climate Collective ASIA for Social and Environmental Impact: Global movement, local collective action
　　【報告者】Mr. Corey Lien (Co-Founder of DOMI, Co-Chairman & Co-Founder of Asia-Pacific B-Corp Association)
　(4) Leading for Responsible Change: Framing Strategies among Taiwanese B Corps
　　【報告者】Associate Prof. Miriam Garvi (College of Management, National Taiwan University)
　　【司　会】谷本寛治教授（早稲田大学商学学術院商学部）

JFBS International Symposium
・日　時　2021 年 1 月 23 日（土）15：00～17：30（JST）
　　　　　　　オンライン（Zoom）
・テーマ・報告者等
　(1) Sustainability and Management in the Post COVID-19 Era
　　【報告者】Jung Wan Lee, PhD, KOREA (Professor, School of International Economics and Trade, Anhui University of Finance and Economics, China; former Professor at Boston University)

(2) Mitigating Pandemic Risks: The Role of Ethics

【報告者】Maxim Storchevoy, PhD, RUSSIA (Associate Professor, HSE University / Director of Russian Business Ethics Network)

(3) The Impact of COVID-19 on Commerce and Sustainability Southeast Asia

【報告者】Daniel McFarlane, PhD, THAILAND (Director, MA in Social Innovation & Sustainability, School of Global Studies, Thammasat University)

(4) Collaboration is one of the KEYS during Pandemic

【報告者】Juniati Gunawan, PhD, INDONESIA (Director, Trisakti Sustainability Center, Trisakti University – Jakarta, Indonesia)

(5) Think of Sustainability in the Pandemic Time

【報告者】Niven Huang, PhD, TAIWAN (Regional Leader of KPMG Sustainability Services in Asia Pacific, KPMG Sustainability Consulting Co., Ltd.)

【Moderator】Kanji Tanimoto, PhD, JAPAN (Professor, School of Commerce, Waseda University / President, JFBS)

JFBS シンポジウム

・日　時　2021 年 3 月 6 日（土）13：30〜16：00

　　　　　オンライン（Zoom）

・テーマ　日本におけるポストコロナと持続可能な「企業と社会」

・パネリスト

　今津秀紀氏（凸版印刷株式会社）

　岡本大輔教授（慶應義塾大学商学部）

　黒田かをり氏（一般財団法人 CSO ネットワーク）

　関正雄氏（損害保険ジャパン株式会社）

　福川恭子教授（一橋大学大学院経営管理研究科）

　【司　会】谷本寛治教授（早稲田大学商学学術院商学部）

第 33 回東日本部会

・日　時　2021 年 5 月 15 日（土）13：30〜16：50（JST）

　　　　　オンライン（Zoom）

・テーマ・報告者等

(1) Workforce wellbeing and CSR strategies: Perspective of managers in large Japanese companies（日本語で報告）

【報告者】小林一紀講師（Management, Entrepreneurship & Innovation at Massey University, New Zealand）

(2) CSR 活動と安定保有株主，株式持ち合い

【報告者】吉田賢一招聘研究員（早稲田大学ビジネス・ファイナンス研究センター）

(3) Improving sustainability management performance using Blockchain technology

【報告者】Prof. Michele John (Director of the Sustainable Engineering Group at Curtin University, Australia)

【司　会】福川恭子教授（一橋大学大学院経営管理研究科）

2.　第 10 回年次大会（2021 年 9 月 2〜3 日）案内

・日　　程　　2021 年 9 月 2 日（木）〜3 日（金）
　　　　　　　オンライン（Zoom）
・主　　催　　企業と社会フォーラム
・本大会プログラム委員会
　　　　　　　Valentina Carbone (Professor, ESCP, Paris, France)
　　　　　　　Michele John (Professor, Curtin University, Australia)
　　　　　　　谷本寛治（早稲田大学教授）
　　　　　　　西尾チヅル（筑波大学大学院教授）
・テ ー マ　　「サーキュラーエコノミーを目指して」

　　生産―消費―廃棄，これは伝統的な産業モデルであり，これまでのビジネスはこのモデルで行われてきました。しかしこの直線的なモデルはもはや持続可能ではなくなっています。Ellen MacArthur Foundation などは，資源やエネルギー消費と経済成長を切り離し，実行可能で再生可能な循環型経済（サーキュラーエコノミー）を提唱しています。サーキュラーエコノミーでは，廃棄物となったものが他のバリューチェーンの資源となること，生産から消費そして廃棄に至るまでの商品ライフサイクルのすべての段階で，いま使われているものを最大限利用していこうとしています。

　　サーキュラーエコノミーのビジネスモデルに関する文献では，廃棄物のリサイクル戦略（循環をつくる）や商品寿命を伸ばすためのエコ開発（循環のスピードを緩める）が多く論じられてきました。また高い耐久性による消費サイクルの長期化，所有に代わって必要な時に利用することや，デジタルプラットフォームを通じた商品の再循環の支援といったシェアリングエコノミーのように，従来とは異なる方法によって循環スピードを緩めることが議論されています。

　　世界が直面している危機的な気候変動や資源不足，廃棄問題のもと，各国では循環型の事業イニシアティブを活性化させ，直線的なモデルを一部の戦略的なものに限定し，サーキュラーエコノミーへ移行することを促す法規制づくりが進められています。

　　2021 年 JFBS 年次大会では，サーキュラーエコノミーの理論構築と実践に向けた議論を進めていきます。サーキュラーエコノミーはどのように周辺の概念やパラダイム，例えばサステナビリティや産業エコロジー（産業における資源やエネルギーの流れ），パーマカルチャー（持続可能な農業・文化），シェアリングエコノミーに影響を及ぼすのか？　われわれは，サーキュラーエコノミーにかかわるテーマを学際的に考えるとともに，これまでのそしてこれからの議論と具体的な取り組みについて考えていきます。主に以下のようなトピックが挙げられます（但しこの限りではありません）。

1.　サーキュラーエコノミーにかかわる政策と戦略。サーキュラーエコノミーへの移行はどのような規制や制度によって可能になるか？　どのような公共政策が地域レベル，国家レベル，国際レベルでサーキュラーエコノミーの発展を促すか？　企業はどのようにサーキュラーエコノミーの概念を戦略に組み込んでいくのか？

2.　サーキュラーエコノミーを促進する企業家精神。サーキュラーエコノミーの分野における企業家精神とは何か？　彼らは地域，国家，国際的にどのようにサーキュラーエコノミーに取り組んでいるのか？

3.　新しい消費パターンとサーキュラーエコノミー。サーキュラーエコノミーの発展に向け

た消費者の行動やモチベーションについて。

4. 関連テーマとして，サステナブル・ファッション，食品ロス，プラスチック問題への取り組み，シェアリング（車，自転車，場所など），持続可能な農業，再生可能エネルギーなどが考えられる。

多くの参加者の皆様によって，新しい議論が提起されることを期待しています。

・主な内容　　＜ Keynote Speech ＞

・R. Edward Freeman (Professor, Darden School of Business, University of Virginia, USA)

・Valentina Carbone (Professor, ESCP, Paris, France)

・Marjut Hannonen (Minister-Counsellor, Head, Delegation of the European Union to Japan)

・Tomomi Fukumoto (Executive Officer, Division COO, Corporate Sustainability Division, Suntory Holdings)

＜ Plenary Session ＞

・Marjut Hannonen (Minister-Counsellor, Head, Delegation of the European Union to Japan)

・Tomomi Fukumoto (Executive Officer, Division COO, Corporate Sustainability Division, Suntory Holdings)

・Izumi Sato (Lawyer)

・Michele John (Professor, Faculty of Science and Technology, Curtin University, Australia)

＜企画セッション＞

1. 廃プラスチック問題① 「プラスチック資源循環の課題と可能性」

2. 食品ロス問題 「プラットフォーム・ビジネスによる食品ロス問題の解決」

3. サステナブル・ファッション 「Sustainable Fashion：3R (Recycle, Reuse, Reduce) and C (Certification) in the fashion industry」

4. 廃プラスチック問題② 「プラスチック資源循環への具体的なアプローチ」

最新の詳細プログラムは，学会ウエブサイトを参照ください。

https://j-fbs.jp/annualconf_2021.html

【Notes for Contributors】

1. The annals mainly consists of invited paper, research paper and case study/general review. For submission to the annals, membership requirement does not apply.

2. Contributions should be original papers written in either Japanese or English on the theme of the JFBS annual conference in that year or topics related to business and society. The contributions have neither been published previously nor are under review for publication elsewhere by the end of September when the annals comes out.

3. Japan Forum of Business and Society (JFBS) has all copyrights of submitted papers for publication.

4. Authors are requested to seek written permission in advance when citing their accepted papers in any other publication including internet sites. With the request accepted, authors cite the annals information such as the series number and the date of publication.

5. All papers are to be submitted in a single column format. Research paper in Japanese language should be no longer than 20,000 characters (case study/general review: 10,000 characters) including title, abstract, keywords, notes, references, tables and figures. Research paper in English should be no longer than 8,000-11,000 words (case study/general review: 4,000-6,000 words) including title, abstract, keywords, notes, references, tables and figures.

6. References should be cited in the text either in brackets, e.g. *Earlier studies (Schumpeter, 1934) showed*···or as part of a sentence, e.g. *Schumpeter (1934) states*···. The reference should be listed alphabetically in the end of papers. In submitted papers, authors should not cite their own previous papers.

7. Authors should attach a cover letter which includes the title of the paper, author(s)' name(s), author(s)' contact information, an abstract (100 to 150 words) and keywords (10 words or phrases) in a word format.

8. Authors should follow the guidelines posted at the JFBS site to ensure their submission is in the correct format. (It is particularly important that authors may not use any third-party material such as figures and images on the internet and photos without appropriate permissions.)

9. Submission deadline for the research paper and case study/general review is January 15th after the annual conference, and for the invited paper, the end of March.

10. The annals uses a double-blind peer review system, in which two referees delegated by the JFBS editorial committee review. Then, the chief editor makes a final decision.

11. When accepted, authors can proofread for publication only once. Neither adding nor deleting sentences/ words can be made while proofreading. Only typographical/literal errors could be corrected.

12. All materials along with submitted papers are not returned to authors for any reason.

13. Papers should be submitted in a word file to info@j-fbs.jp
    Tel & Fax: +81-3-3203-7132   E-mail: info@j-fbs.jp   URL: https://j-fbs.jp
    Japan Forum of Business and Society (JFBS)
    c/o: Tanimoto Office, School of Commerce, Waseda University,
    1-6-1 Nishiwaseda, Shinjyuku-Ku, Tokyo 169-8050, Japan

Japan Forum of Business and Society Annals, No.10

Edited by Japan Forum of Business and Society
Published by Chikura Publishing

Index

企業と社会フォーラム学会誌

【企業と社会シリーズ10】

2021年9月1日　発行

編　者　企業と社会フォーラム

発行者　千倉成示

発行所　株式会社　千倉書房
　　　　〒104-0031　東京都中央区京橋2-4-12
　　　　Tel 03-3273-3931　Fax 03-3273-7668
　　　　https://www.chikura.co.jp/

印刷／製本　藤原印刷

表紙デザイン　さくらい　ともか